The Prop Master

A guidebook for successful theatrical prop management

Amy Mussman

illustrated by James Mussman

MERIWETHER PUBLISHING LTD.
Colorado Springs, Colorado

Meriwether Publishing Ltd., Publisher
PO Box 7710
Colorado Springs, CO 80933-7710

www.meriwether.com

Editor: Arthur L. Zapel
Assistant Editor: Audrey Scheck
Cover design: Jan Melvin
Cover and interior illustrations: James Mussman

Library of Congress Cataloging-in-Publication Data

Mussman, Amy.
  The prop master : a guidebook for successful theatrical prop management / by Amy Mussman; illustrated by James Mussman.
    p. cm.
Includes bibliographical references.
ISBN 978-1-56608-154-2 (pbk.)
1. Stage props. I. Title.
  PN2091.S8M84 2008
  792.02'5--dc22
                          2007049714

1   2   3   08   09   10

Contents

What's in this book anyway?
What page is it on?
Help!

Special Thanks 1

Introduction 3

Chapter 1: What Are Props? 5

Chapter 2: The Prop Master 15

Chapter 3: Interacting with Other People 26

Chapter 4: A Successful Work Environment 36

Chapter 5: The Prop Shop 46

Chapter 6: Collections and Files 78

Chapter 7: The First Steps of the Build Process 92

Chapter 8: Start "Propping" 109

Chapter 9: Rehearsals and Performances 120

Chapter 10: Safety 141

Chapter 11: Timeless Tips and Techniques 152

Basic Theater Terminology: A Glossary of Sorts 163

Bibliography and Resources 181

About the Author 183

About the Illustrator 185

Special Thanks

Nothing is possible in regards to anything "theater," even the creation of a book, without the help of a wonderful community of people. So, for those who graciously trained and mentored me, set aside your time to offer theatrical insight, writing advice, or who have just helped out in other countless ways to make this book possible, I offer my deepest appreciation. I love you so much.

Thank you:
James Mussman, Illustrator
Mike and Phyllis Mussman
John and Thea Mussman;
Colin, Kara, Kristin

Kate Anderson	Sarah Baptist
Meghan Brodie	David Centers
Kristina Chadwick	Marie Chiment
Charles Conway	Anne Conwell
Rebecca Frederick	Dan and Tina Gaffney
Melanie Garvin	Jim Guy
Mark Hamberger	Stefanie Hansen
Libbie Hawes	Mara Hyatt
Marla Jurglanis	Kathi Kacinski
Tara Knowles	Robert Kovarik
Kay Longo	Devon Lovell
Katie Lozier	Robin Lu Payne

1

Marci Maullar
Beth Ohlsson
Britt Plunkett
Rachel Shane, Ph.D.
John Uthoff
Mark Wethington
Shannon Zura

Tiina Nunnally
Mark O'Maley
Eric and Susan Schaeffer
Marka Suber
Mindy Waugh
Nicole Wisbey

Society of Property Artisan Managers
Kansas State University
Eastpoint Community Church
Delaware Theater Company
Maine State Music Theater

Introduction

Congratulations! You are a prop master! You have entered the realm where art, science, the present, the past, technology, magic, and imagination boil together as ingredients of extraordinary creation. But wait! There's much more to this majestic profession than reveling in the glory of making and supplying props for a production.

Why Read This Book?

During the past ten years of working as a prop master for professional theater houses and as a freelance prop artisan, I have not come across a book that is truly geared toward helping a prop master figure out what his job is really about. Other than a few books which offered a small chapter on theatrical properties or suggested a basic definition of the prop master as simply "someone who supplies props for a production," there was nothing available to those of us who wanted to learn more on how to perfect our responsibilities. When I first became a prop master, I was full of questions about what I was supposed to do (besides prop a show) and how to go about it. Except for books on how to make props (which really are wonderful, useful, and invaluable in their own right), I had no resources or guides to turn to for answers. I had to figure out the full load of responsibilities and expectations of my supervisors, co-workers, and designers through trial and error, *and* I had to prop a show on top of it all. Nowadays, my preliminary propping processes and communication skills are habits, but I've recently encountered a lot of volunteer, first-time, freelance, and budding professional prop masters who have posed the question: "How do you work as a prop master on a regular basis without losing your mind?" The answer is not simple; it is rather complex. Thus, there is a need for an entire book encompassing the craft of the prop master.

Whether you are a professional, volunteer, or student prop master, this book will take you through the necessary steps of thought and action needed to be a top-notch properties master in the theatrical world. If you are a prop artisan, like to dabble in props, or just want to understand the inner workings of an important technical theater position, you are in the right place. This guidebook focuses on describing the duties of a prop master that are above and beyond the actual build processes of a properties department and will help you understand the importance of being a well-prepared, knowledgeable member of any production team.

Universal Application

The information provided in this book is based on a standard model of professional theater and the qualifications expected of a professional prop master. When it comes to producing a show, most institutions emulate the processes, positions, requirements, and schedules of professional theater. Aspects of production and performance are the same, despite the differing frameworks of each organization or level of expertise. Therefore, the processes and strategies outlined in this book are universal and can be applied to every prop master in any production environment.

Chapter 1
What Are Props?

"You know — props are those things that cover the stage set and the actors carry them around sometimes ..." That's just the start of the definition of props. Stage Properties, or props, help with telling the story of the play. Props are tangible items — things that enhance and create the location of the setting. Props play an important role in helping to define the personality of every character while assisting with the action in the play.

What Do Props Do?

Stage props are a big deal for theater productions. Props may look like lifeless things, but they are full of soul and have a duty to the production they serve. Faithfully, props defend the believability, credibility, and spirit of the production. Props are inanimate objects that magically bring definition and personality to the fictional environmental setting in which they reside. They are distinguished costume accessories that embellish the dispositions of the portrayed characters. Props support the dramatic nature of the play and are convincing narrators who help to transform a two-dimensional tale into a physical and undeniably real place and time.

Props don't appear by their own volition. They are intentionally chosen as important elements of the production written into the script and specifically designed to enhance the setting. Props are acquired for each show by the prop master who, after much research and planning, decides if each piece will be built, bought, borrowed, or found.

Prop Categories

The sky is the limit when it comes to determining what things could be props. From peas to helicopters, props range in size, shape, style, and purpose. In an effort to make it easier to reference the millions of various props in the world, props are assigned to three categories: **Hand Props, Set Props,** and **Set Dressing Props.** These three categories distinguish props by the different jobs they do or roles they play during a performance and help prioritize their importance during the propping process. Knowing which categories props fall into becomes important when you are creating your props and to-do lists and communicating with members of the production team.

Creative Teams

Throughout this chapter, the various prop categories are discussed in detail. Included in the discussion is a list of production team members that prop masters can look to for information regarding certain props. I refer to these groups of people as the "creative teams." Each creative team list is meant to give you an idea as to who helps make prop decisions and who might be asked to help answer prop questions or provide more information.

Again, this is just a guide, and it may not apply to the circumstances at your theater.

The creative teams are included with each category because sharing information and asking and answering questions can be confusing during the production process. When I was a first-time prop master, it took me awhile to figure out who was affected by or involved in the procurement of props. Obviously the lighting designer won't care about all the practical props in a show — just the ones that light up. The stage manager rarely makes prop decisions, but will always be involved in sharing and relaying prop information. The set designer and director have the right to change, add, or cut props as they see fit. Every theater and production is different, and your best judgment will usually lead you to the right person for help.

Hand Props

Hand props are things actors use or touch, pick up, or carry in a production. With the exception of props hidden within pockets, these props are usually not worn. Hand props are small to medium in size and are usually not secured to the set. Usually deemed as high priority, hand props are personal to the actor and specific to the character the actor is portraying. Either they debut from offstage, having been preset on backstage prop tables, or they are specifically placed on-stage at the start of each act or scene.

Creative Team: Director, Actors, Set Designer

Examples of Hand Props: Books, Brooms, Coffee Mugs, Flasks, Keys, Lanterns, Letters, Luggage, Money, Phones, Tools, Toys, Trophies, Weapons, Musical instruments.

Hand Prop Subcategories

Based on the multifarious functions hand props perform, they can be further divided and placed into subcategories. These subcategories are referenced often in technical theater by the production departments that have direct involvement with the function or look of these props. The subcategories are: **Consumable Props, Costume Props, Manual/Special Effects Props,** and **Practical Props**.

At the risk of making matters more confusing, props often cross category and subcategory lines. For example, an actress' handbag which suffers the ill fate of being ripped to shreds at some point in the show would fall under the following categories and subcategories: Hand Prop (the bag is handled by an actor), Costume Prop (the bag would accessorize the costume), and Special Effects Prop (the bag would need to be rigged to rip easily). Amazing, huh? On the brighter side, knowing the categories and subcategories that props fall into will make you look like a smart prop master who is interested and involved in the craft of propping. Additionally, this vocabulary will make communicating with production department heads and guest artists easier and more efficient.

Consumable Props

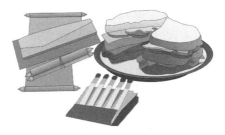

Consumable props are actually hand props which get eaten, beaten, or broken and will need replacing on a regular basis. *Consumables*, for short, can take a chunk out of the prop budget, and enough money should be set aside for these props well before the prop materials budget is depleted.

Consumable food props are eaten during the show and need to be fresh at the start of each performance. Actors should be able to rest assured that the food they are consuming is fresh and edible, not past its prime. Food poisoning has serious consequences. The whole production, including your reputation, can suffer if an actor gets sick. The prop department is responsible for supplying fresh ingredients for these consumable props throughout the run of the show. At most theaters, it is usually the running crew who prepares the food for consumption.

Creative Team: Stage Management, Director, Set Designer
Examples: Beverages, Meals, Candy, Fruits, Veggies, Fake Pills

Consumable props which are broken, torn, or crumpled purposefully during action of play will need new replacements before the start of the next performance. If your theater is planning on having twenty paid performances, you will need, at the very least, twenty prop replacements *plus* enough replacements to get through rehearsals, dress rehearsals, and preview performances.

Creative Team: Stage Management, Director, Set Designer, Actors
Examples: Paper Products, Dish and Glassware, Knick-knacks

Consumable props that take a beating during the run of performances will need to be refreshed every few performances. These are props that can get away with looking aged for a short time before they may start disintegrating or items that will just be used up over time.

Creative Team: Stage Management, Director, Set Designer
Examples: Love letters, Candles, Matches, Business Cards

Costume Props

Costume props are items actors wear or carry that complete a costume. These kinds of props help the audience understand who a character is and what he is like. Most often, these props are supplied by the prop department, but there are cases when the costume department prefers to garner these special accessories. As these types of props are requested  — either before or during the rehearsal process — coordinate with the costume designer and costume shop manager as to which department would like to assume the responsibility of finding these lovely articles.

Creative Team: Director, Costume Designer, Costume Shop

Examples: Briefcases, Canes, Guns, Holsters, Jewelry, Keys, Masks, Purses, Swords

Manual Effects/ Special Effects Props

Manual and special effect props have a trick to them and are used or operated in a way that is potentially dangerous or unconventional in the real world. These props need special care and should be locked up, cleaned up, or picked up at the end of every use and must be reset before the next use. The manual or special effect could be operated by either the actor or stage crew member. Oftentimes, live sound cues are produced with offstage props.

Creative Team: Stage Management, Director, Designer, Production Staff

Examples: Burning crucifixes, Burnt meatloaf, Campfires, Crash boxes, Exploding clocks, Gunshots, Magic tricks, Neck snaps, Rats that ooze blood, and much, much more

Practical Props

Practical props are usually set dressing or hand props that need electricity or battery power to operate. "Practicals" are adapted or designed to work as they would in everyday life. A table lamp that is practical will be plugged into an electrical source, have the ability to turn on, and light up during the show. Props such as lanterns or candles are adapted as battery-operated practicals simulated to glow like live flame (most theaters opt not to use live flame to avoid potential fire hazards). A kitchen or bathroom sink that produces water from the faucet is also considered a practical prop, even though the plumbing is not the same as in a true building.

Creative Team: Set and Light Designer, Director, Production Staff

Examples: Candles, Chandeliers, Lamps, Lanterns, Ringing phones, Running water, Stoves, Toasters

Set Props

Set props serve dual purposes; they adorn the set and serve the actors. In realistic settings, set props are usually stationary furniture pieces that remain in the same location on-stage throughout the entire scene. These props vary in size, type, and function, and are chosen to define the location of the play and to reflect the historical time period and economic status of the story and characters. To clarify, set *pieces* are sometimes used, sat on, or manipulated by the actors in the same way as set *props*; however, set pieces are purposely designed scenic elements, built by the set department and, in most cases, permanently attached to certain areas of the set.

Creative Team: Set Designer, Director, Actors

Examples: Appliances, Beds, Benches, Boulders, Couches, Crates, End tables, Microwaves, Pianos, Refrigerators, Rolling carts, Stoves

Set Dressing

Set dressing is the collection of props that defines the setting or environment of the play. These props are usually for decoration only and remain stationary during scenes. Although these items do not have an imperative use, they play an important role in setting the stage and assisting the audience with understanding the world they are viewing. The script and set designs are the keys for helping you picture how the setting should look. The set designer and director have a huge say in what types of dressing should be sought after and how pristine or distressed these props will look. Set dressing is important, but is usually low on the priority list.

Creative Team: Set Designer, Director, Stage Management

Examples: Baskets of fruit, Books, Electronics, Curtains, Dishes, Knickknacks, Pictures, Plants, Pots and pans, Rugs, Small kitchen appliances, Wall hangings

11

Prop Importance

The Actor's Friend

Actors rely on props. When you are the prop master, you are actively involved with helping the actors practice their jobs from day one. As artists, actors need access to all mediums which create and influence their work. Props are to actors what canvas, paint, and paintbrush are to painters. Just like with a visual artist, the actor can imagine and dream his masterpiece, but without his tools and supplies, most of his visual creation will be lost on the audience.

Actors like props; props become the actor's wingman and vice versa as they both look out for each other. An actor who is introduced to a new prop will usually require an adjustment period, but the actor and prop will soon become fast friends.

Blocking

Props affect blocking, and blocking affects props. *Blocking* refers to the staged movements an actor is given by the director during the course of the play. Actors are blocked or staged according to how the set is designed and where props are placed. The actors' movements become nearly habitual once learned. As actors become more comfortable with their surroundings on-stage, even the slightest change to a prop can potentially distract an actor or throw off the timing of his movements. This applies to nearly every prop an actor must manipulate. The prop master works with stage management to acclimate the actors to each new prop introduced during the rehearsal process.

Character and Setting Definition

Props bridge the gap between scenery and costumes by establishing, unifying, and tying together the design elements and the artistic concept of the production.

Props provide the audience with a more tangible understanding of the story. All props establish:

• The mood and feeling of the play.
• The socioeconomic status and personality of the characters who live among them.
• The time of year.
• The period of history.
• The real and imaginary.

Every single prop needs to be appropriate to the show. Every prop has a purpose, is specially chosen to be a part of the production, and actively gives life to and defines the space around it.

Props and Other Departments

Props can affect the workload and emotional state of other production team members as well as yourself. The props you choose are based on specific details. A table lamp might seem like an easy thing to find, yet it needs to fit the time period of the show, be short enough for the audience to see an actor standing behind it, have a shade that matches the color of the sofa, and be controlled by the light board. Already, you are seeking the attention of many production team members. The director has final say in all things regarding his show's concept, appearance, and function. The set designer focuses on how the style of the lamp works within the concept and design of the show. The electric department wires the prop properly (if you haven't done so already) and connects it to the lighting system. The light designer chews his nails over whether or not the lamp will produce enough light. And, finally, the costume department worries that the costume designer will freak out because the lamp shade (and, of course, the sofa) are the same color as the lead actor's costume.

An Excellent Stock of Props

During downtime and in between acting gigs, props like to rest and spend time with their fellow props. A storeroom with a healthy stock of stuff is a great vacation spot for tired props. It's a tough job being a prop, and no one understands that more than the prop master.

A basic stock of props should include:

Armchairs	Artificial flowers	Artificial food
Artificial plants	Bags	Bar equipment
Barrels	Baskets	Beds (twin & full)
Bed Linen	Benches	Blankets
Books	Bookcases	Breakfront
Brooms	Buckets	Candlesticks
Canes	Canteens	Cash registers
Cast iron cookware	Chaise	Chandeliers
China sets	Chests	Coat trees

The prop master wears many hats. You probably already knew that; it *is* a common saying amongst prop masters. And it's true: every project requires an old skill and presents the need to learn a new one. In one work day, your duties could range from office manager to clock maker to welder to carpet cleaner to receptionist to graphic artist to ... the list goes on.

Inspired by a friend's T-shirt concerning the various roles a bartender assumes when fraternizing with customers, I created this a few years ago:

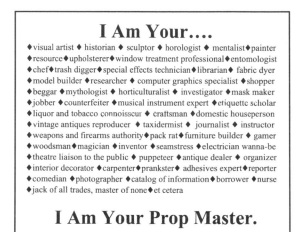

I Am Your....

◆visual artist ◆ historian ◆ sculptor ◆ horologist ◆ mentalist◆painter ◆resource◆upholsterer◆window treatment professional◆entomologist ◆chef◆trash digger◆special effects technician◆librarian◆ fabric dyer ◆model builder ◆researcher ◆ computer graphics specialist ◆shopper ◆beggar ◆mythologist ◆ horticulturalist ◆ investigator ◆mask maker ◆jobber ◆counterfeiter ◆musical instrument expert ◆etiquette scholar ◆liquor and tobacco connoisseur ◆ craftsman ◆domestic houseperson ◆vintage antiques reproducer ◆ taxidermist ◆ journalist ◆ instructor ◆weapons and firearms authority◆pack rat◆furniture builder ◆ gamer ◆woodsman◆magician ◆inventor ◆seamstress ◆electrician wanna-be ◆theatre liaison to the public ◆ puppeteer ◆antique dealer ◆ organizer ◆interior decorator ◆carpenter◆prankster◆ adhesives expert◆reporter ◆comedian ◆photographer ◆catalog of information◆borrower ◆nurse ◆jack of all trades, master of none◆et cetera

I Am Your Prop Master.

The propping business is an odd one, jumping from one task to another as you go about your business, not realizing how odd it is to the average person that you could spend your lunch hour demonstrating theatrical blood techniques to an elementary school and then drive back to your office to clean a gun and make several baggies full of illegal drug props for the upcoming original one-act play festival. It's no wonder prop masters are in such high demand.

You are a visual storyteller. You work right alongside the director and the designer to tell the story of the play to the audience. You are a partner with an equally vested interest in the success of the design. It is your skills and talents that are displayed as the story's physical narrators.

The Prop Department

The good news is that most theater organizations have finally hit a turning point in recognizing the prop department as a legitimate branch of technical production. (Insert applause.) For whatever reason, it has taken the majority of the theater industry a long time to view "Props" as a fully functioning operation, independent of the scene shop. This is not to say that the prop and scene shops no longer need to collaborate; however, theaters have begun to eliminate the technical director as the "middle man" involved in prop business. The prop master is seen as the true manager, the official head of the department, reporting to the production manager in line with other production department heads.

Positions

A perfect prop department would have a staff of several artisans who collectively bring a wide range of skills to the table. The work of a prop staff could free up time for the prop master so he could properly manage the department, talk with designers and directors, attend rehearsals, and sit in on all of the tech rehearsals. Yet, most prop masters either work alone or with a much smaller staff, assuming all the duties within the department themselves.

Prop Master

Prop masters have varying titles depending on the preferences of their organizations. Some of the different titles are: Prop Master, Properties Master, Properties Manager, Props Mistress, Prop Supervisor, Prop Director, and Properties Designer.

The basic job description of the prop master remains roughly the same no matter the title, varying only slightly depending on your organization and its needs. Regardless of the mundane nature of the job description, which does not properly exemplify every treasure of the job, the responsibilities are still weighty and should be followed to the letter. Here is a sample job description:

The prop master will carry out all of these primary duties and responsibilities and will report directly to the production manager:

1. Supply all rehearsal and performance props for every production through appropriate planning and procuring methods.
2. Read each play and develop a cost breakdown list and prop list for each production.
3. Work with designers and directors on creating and acquiring each prop in accordance with the production design and concept.
4. Coordinate prop needs with stage management including fulfilling all prop requests for the production.
5. Meet deadlines as discussed per production.
6. Load all props into the stage space and work with designer to organize set dressing work.
7. Coordinate any scheduling, load-in, or prop needs with appropriate production department heads.
8. Attend all production and full staff meetings.
9. Attend all technical rehearsals, dress rehearsals, preview performances, and the notes sessions following.
10. Ensure the safety and maintenance of all props for each production from acquisition through strike.
11. Organize and supervise all prop-related office and work spaces, prop storage areas, and prop stock, including all supplies and tools.
12. Keep accurate records of all expenditures. Stay within allotted budget amount. Turn in all receipts and time sheets to finance department in a timely fashion.
13. Manage and supervise prop department staff and hire artisans.
14. Coordinate and handle the rental of all theater properties.

Assistant Prop Master

The assistant prop master should be trained to handle any of the above duties of the prop master should she ever need to assume this job responsibility. The assistant reports to the prop master, yet has some supervisory responsibilities to other prop department staff. The assistant performs a wide range of propping and building tasks.

Prop Artisan

Prop artisans report to the assistant and/or the prop master and come with any number of titles and skill sets. Depending on the theater, an artisan may be hired to perform many propping and building duties, or she may be assigned to a specific area. An artisan's area of expertise is usually reflected in her title, which could be one of the following: Prop Carpenter, Shopper/Buyer, and Soft Goods and Small Crafts Specialists.

Staff Management

A prop master lucky enough to have a staff of one or more needs to realize his fortune and utilize his artisans to the best of his capacity. A happy working environment will produce the best creative inspirations and propping results.

Training and Supervising

Every prop department, no matter how innovative, must not only set prop quality expectations, but also follow theater rules and policies.

Theater, like any other art, encourages growth and supports all learning processes that benefit the production and experience of the artists. Training your staff to continue to learn and gather new skills while improving the old will take your entire department to the next level.

Delegating and Trusting

Share propping projects with those who have the skill to do the job properly, but trust that the project can also be completed by someone who may not possess the skill but is eager to give it a go. Pass along all pertinent information for a project when you assign tasks so that the props are built or acquired correctly the first time and no one winds up feeling like a fool or looking like a jerk.

Guiding and Acknowledging

Guide your staff toward positive thinking, a collective team effort, and a supportive environment. Acknowledge your staff for their accomplishments, and meet with them privately when concerned with improvements. Pass along kudos, compliments, and thanks that you hear but your staff may not. Always demonstrate gratitude and encouragement.

Technical Skills

The prop master is a "jack of all trades." You probably already know that, too. A jack of all trades who wears many hats — we are busy!

No prop master is born knowing how to do everything or liking everything he has to do. Therefore you should not be deterred from pursuing a one-time gig or a full-time career in props if you don't know how to sew and hate shopping. Possessing a multitude of skills increases your credentials, but having the courage and interest to learn, learn, and keep learning will really make you succeed in this business. Most prop masters have gained their skills through on-the-job experience and trial and error. Each prop master has his strengths and weaknesses just like the other guy. What makes you stand out as a prop master is that you do not let your weaknesses or performance handicaps keep you from accomplishing tasks.

In addition to the hats you wear and the roles you play, there are many skills of the trade that are involved in propping processes. Not all skills are used for each show. If you don't know how to do something, you can either learn it or find someone who is willing to do the work for you. Here is a short list of technical know-how the prop department calls forth on a fairly regular basis.

Drafting

Understanding designer plans and materials as well as common symbols and drawing methods is necessary for studying and recording prop data. The prop master will also need to create designs or working drawings from time to time, and knowing how to draft is helpful.

Woodworking

Carpentry and woodworking skills are a necessity. It is rare for a prop master not to have to build something out of wood for a production. If this isn't your cup of tea, tell yourself you need to learn and start slowly with easy projects.

Sewing

From hand sewing to machine work, lots of soft goods are created in the prop shop — pillows, curtains, upholstery work, etc.

Painting

From fine art to scenic art, the prop master will befriend his paintbrush. Painting skills improve with practice and patience.

Crafting

Crafting projects require a creative problem-solving mentality that lets you picture the finished prop and piece together the parts and the process. Crafting encompasses a wide range of arts and crafts from the elementary level to the professional.

Metalworking

Welding and soldering are important skills to learn..

Graphic Arts

Computer programs are a lifesaver for the prop shop and absolutely eliminate the old-school process of cutting and pasting. Learn how to create documents and spreadsheets and how to work with imaging programs. You'll be grateful for this kind of training.

Researching

If you don't know what something is supposed to look like, how are you supposed to go out and get it? Conducting research is a must in the prop shop.

Shopping

This is not every prop master's favorite activity, and some just don't possess the skills. If this duty falls on your shoulders, just smile and get it done.

Training

If you can take classes which enhance your skills in these various trades, do! Otherwise, practice these skills when you have the opportunity. No one is born knowing how to do everything, but desire and willingness to learn will keep you working.

Personal Attributes

It is fascinating how your view of the world and all that surrounds you changes when you become a prop master. Realistic, everyday scenes that you may have taken for granted, or which seemed mundane or typical, jump out at you as enthralling. The way different upholstery fabrics and wooden frames wear out on furniture will catch your eye. The stuff that clutters coffee tables, is hung on the fridge, or is forgotten in your medicine cabinet will turn into the perfect prop-dressing reference. The various coloring and garnishing of a roasted chicken becomes something that you study rather than crave. Before you know it, the historical "why, when, and how" of things will delight you like never before.

In addition to having personality traits that cause you to adopt aspects of your job and subconsciously apply them to everyday life, a good prop master will possess a multitude of positive personal attributes. These features and characteristics are doubly important for you to carry around because they benefit the different kinds of work you do and the networks you need to maintain. When you are a team player and enjoy working in a collaborative and creative environment, the rest of these important attributes will fall into place.

A good prop master should possess and demonstrate these attributes:

Accepts Responsibility — is proactive in taking on new projects and dependable with following through until the end.

Balance — is able to address managerial and creative issues well.

Business Mind — knows the importance of staying within budget.

Common Sense — knows how to stay safe, when and when not to do something or make a decision.

Creative Problem Solving — can explore all aspects of a project and use common or unconventional methods or materials to tackle the problem.

Creativity — possesses artistic talent, likes to make things and come up with plans.

Attention to Detail — being able to see the trees within the forest makes a production that much tighter.

Flexibility — can change plans with a good attitude.

Pleasantness/Attitude — remains friendly and leaves problems at the door; won't drag others down when feeling low.

Good Memory — remembers what people have said, is mindful of the schedule, and can picture where something is.

Knowledge of Theater — either has previous technical experience or possesses a passion for it.

Networking — is a great advocate for the theater.

Openness — shares information appropriately and consistently and involves others in discussions and problem solving; accepts new people, situations, and ideas.

Organization — has a plan of attack, keeps spaces and information clean and tidy.

Self-Teaching — seeks out ways to educate self and is willing to try and try again.

Toughness — is physically strong, demonstrates perseverance, knows how to handle problems and deal with tough situations.

Prop Etiquette 101

Be that prop master, that theater employee, that co-worker, that theater technician who is known as courteous and professional. You can do your part in keeping the basic rules of etiquette alive and be a model citizen. It won't hurt. I promise.

The Basics

Phone Etiquette

Return business calls within a timely manner. Make any business phone calls during appropriate business hours. If you must make evening calls, do so when you know dinner will be over and bedtime has not begun. Calls before 9:00 AM are usually not appreciated.

Silence your cell phone when you are in a meeting or attending rehearsals or performances.

Leaving the Office

Let people know your plans if you leave the office. Because of the nature of your work, you will be out of the office frequently. Verbally tell your staff or leave a note.

Punctuality

If you have set an appointment, be on time or a few minutes early. If you fear you will be late, notify the person you are meeting.

Being late to a production or staff meeting is forgivable the first time, but starts to look bad or intentional any time after that. Maintain a good reputation.

Appropriate Work Attire

When you perform the kind of work prop masters do, certain outfits either don't work well or are absolutely not appropriate. Women will have a hard time with skirts or dresses unless the day is filled with non-strenuous activities. Sturdy, comfortable shoes, work pants or jeans, and shirts that can withstand dust, paint, dirt, sweat, etc., work the best. Keep long hair tied back. Never wear clothing that could reveal "too much" or be distracting to others.

Send Thank-You Letters

Send a thank-you note to people who have helped you, let you borrow a prop, served you in any way, or given you a great deal.

Respect

Honor other people and their feelings.

Smile. All the time. It will always keep circumstances light and hold you in a perpetually great mood. When you meet someone for the first time, smile and offer your hand for a handshake. Regardless of gender, the firmer the handshake, the more confidence you exude.

When someone else is talking, please pay attention, do not interrupt, and actively listen to what they are saying. If you ask someone a question, listen to their answer.

Admitting Fault

If you hurt someone's feelings or have done a bad deed that caused someone else distress, apologize. Own up to mistakes you made even if they are minor. Do not place blame or fingerpoint, especially if you had involvement in the matter.

Keeping Your Cool

You have a duty as a prop master to supply what props are needed for a performance, even if, in your opinion, the request seems ridiculous. Refrain from sighing or rolling your eyes. If you find fault with someone else's decision or request, discuss the situation calmly and respectfully.

If impatient guest artists supply props without your knowledge or consent, nip the problem in the bud. Nicely, yet firmly, explain that you are in the process of propping the show and, while you thank them for their generosity, you would appreciate having them consult you first.

As a human, you are going to react emotionally to your surroundings. As a prop master, you may encounter a coworker who always brags, a designer who belittles, and/or an actor who is quite demanding. While remaining on firm ground, swallow your pride. Heated arguments, no matter what the circumstances, never produce good results.

Dealing with Stress

When you feel stressed about your workload or when times seem tough, mentally pull yourself out of your work, step away from it, and breathe. What you are ultimately working on is a *play*, not brain surgery. Although people are depending on you or asking you to meet deadlines, they are not asking you to save the world.

You have an interesting job. Have fun with it!

Backstage Etiquette

Unless you are faced with an emergency, there are a few basic rules of being backstage which is second nature to all theater professionals:

* No talking or laughing out loud.
* No eating, drinking, or smoking.
* Tread lightly. No running.
* No peering through the curtains: If you can see audience, the audience can see you.
* Don't touch props that aren't yours.
* Do not cause distractions or break concentration.

Chapter 3
Interacting with Other People

"Why can't I just work alone?" Being a proactive team member is a necessity, and as a prop master you have to work with nearly every department within the theater at any given time. Good relationships and communication will help "grease the gears" and keep the entire organization running smoothly. The alliances the prop master creates within the theater will prove to be beneficial.

The Theater Family

Part of what makes theater a fun field in which to work is the camaraderie and family atmosphere produced by working with other theater professionals. Nothing is more fulfilling than facing a full fifteen-hour rehearsal day knowing you will be surrounded by people who share your same interest, drive, sense of humor, and enthusiasm toward *work*, of all things!

All theaters are just huge families of talented individuals brought together not because of blood ties but because of an enormous passion for the art of theater. The talent within the theater family is widely diverse, as it should be. From those who consider the theater's future and the impact on the community to folks focused on perfecting the tiniest of details, these brilliantly gifted people work side by side for endless amounts of time just to put on a show.

It is inspiring, really, to view the work these family members produce and understand how much heart and soul goes into every task. Their incentive comes from their own personal dedication, love, and interest in seeing a job well done.

Established primarily for entertainment and education, theater is a business, and the bills must be paid. Theaters rely on public awareness and community interest to generate revenue. Ticket sales, monetary donations, and fundraising events help keep the doors open. From backstage to the front office, raising this money falls onto the shoulders of everyone who works in the theatre. If the theater is not producing a quality product, public interest will wane. Regardless of the production quality, the theatre also suffers when the public is not being informed of the events being produced.

The theater family of employees is a powerful machine. When kept well oiled and maintained, all the gears will be in sync, the theater business will prosper, and the community will be enlivened. Just like all the other employees, the prop master is an essential component and member of this theater family.

Theater Organizational Structure

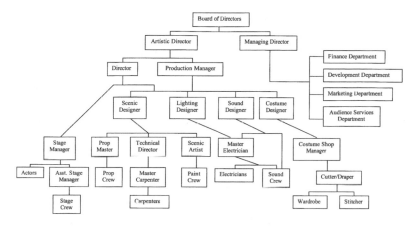

Figure 3.1   *Theater Organization Structure Chart*

Nearly all theaters attempt to assimilate a common organizational structure like the model in Figure 3.1. Theaters range in physical size, budget, and purpose, which affects the various positions and departments within the company. A theater described as "large" usually staffs more people within the departments than the model shown. Smaller theaters have fewer employees who usually double up on responsibilities if possible. Production sizes tend to reflect the theater's size. "Production size" refers to the size of a theater's production budgets, designs, staff, guest artists, and the kinds of shows produced.

Depending on the theater, position titles may vary, or combined positions may assume one job title. The Stage Manager in one theater might be the Production Stage Manager in another. Likewise, the Prop Master might be the Director of Properties, Prop Manager, Properties Supervisor, etc. The Box Office Manager may not only supervise the box office, but also serve as the director of the Audience Services Department. It is an act of courtesy and etiquette for you to know a person's proper title and refer to it correctly. Unintentional confusion between "Director of ..." and "Manager of ..." could cause a huge offense.

Understanding who is who and what they do at your theater is all a part of the job. Naturally, you'll spend most of your time with team members and guest artists in the production departments, but, more often than not, you will rely on the resources and talents of your co-workers in other areas of the theater. Maintaining positive relationships can work both ways: the prop master may be asked to provide services which benefit other departments and support the welfare of the company. It is not unheard of to be asked to participate with fundraising events, help with a mailing, supply props for a window display, and even speak to school groups.

The Relationships

Despite the solidarity of certain projects, the prop master does not work alone. Without the guidance and design of the supervisor, director, and designers, or the support and collaboration from production team members, the prop master would not be able to successfully prop the show. Respecting and honoring those who do their job so you can do yours is an obligation.

The Board of Directors

The Board of Directors is a group of people chosen (based on their personal or professional expertise in varying fields) to help make executive decisions regarding the financial health and overall welfare of the company. The board is involved with the hiring of the artistic director and managing director. With the use of committees, the board requires its members to participate in the affairs and activities of the theater. Oftentimes board members offer their help to prop masters, and prop masters love to have the help of the board, especially when needing to procure props or services that exceed the allowable budget. Board members usually have invaluable contacts in the community whom they can call upon when propping gets tough.

Administrative Departments

People who work in theater administration handle many of the "business" aspects of theater. These offices scout for monetary donors, recruit volunteers, coordinate events, seek new patrons, sign paychecks, and plan the future of the theater company. Each department may be made up of several full-time employees who assist a director or department manager with projects ranging from daily tasks to regular events.

Artistic Director

Appointed by the Board of Directors or a founder of the company, the artistic director makes most of the decisions regarding the theater's artistic vision: choosing plays for the upcoming season, acting as the theater's representative to the community, and approving ideas and materials used in promoting the theater. This person also handles many management duties such as overseeing the work of the production departments, counseling staff, finding creative talent, and being the main contact for budding playwrights and directors. Aside from being one of the prop master's supervisors, the artistic director is known to direct at least one production per theater season.

Managing Director

The managing director reports to the Board of Directors and works in conjunction with the artistic director in theater promotion and fundraising. With the support of many departments, this position is responsible for the financial future of the company while managing daily operations. The prop master can rely on the managing director's community contacts when finding props, and it is usually the managing director who calls upon the prop department for help with events.

Development Department

The development department is responsible for creating and implementing fundraising ideas and events. The people of this department work with the managing director to seek corporate contributions and individual donors. The development department may ask the prop master to designate a prop for a silent auction or assist with other money-making adventures.

Marketing Department

The marketing department is charged with creating a positive and inviting community opinion of the company through promotions, advertising, and maintaining excellent relationships with the press. Always looking for a way to reach out to the community, the marketing department often asks the production team members for help with mailings, display creation, or the coordination of photo sessions and public guest artist interviews.

Financial Department

What good would a job be if not for the reward of a pay check? The financial department manages the theater's revenue. This includes making deposits, paying the bills, and offering advice on financial matters while keeping a close eye on the amount of funds available and how the theater's money is being used. In some theaters the director of finance also serves as the unofficial human resource manager, handling tax and insurance information. The prop master provides the finance department with receipts for expenditures, reimbursements, and any other information or transactions.

Audience Services Department

The audience services department is comprised of a group of people devoted to providing excellent customer service to the theater's guests and patrons while acting as sales representatives. This department is usually comprised of the box office and house management staff, including volunteer ushers and custodial staff. This department can be generous with the prop master regarding free tickets needed to barter with a vendor.

Daily Communication

Within any given day, the prop master could have some form of communication with at least fifteen different people. Amazing, huh? It's true. There are those days when it feels like nothing is getting done because of having to talk to so many people. However, conversing equals information sharing, and if you think about it that way, you've had a pretty productive work day.

To visualize just how many people the prop master communicates with daily, take a gander at figure 3.2.

Daily Communication Tree for Prop Master

Figure 3.2

Production Departments and Team Members

The prop master is the head of the prop department and shares the responsibility of coordinating schedules, communicating needs and information, and participating in the collective creative process with other production department heads, team members, and guest artists.

Production Manager

The production manager oversees the work and affairs of every member and guest of the production department. This person provides pertinent budget information, creates the season production calendar, and solves a multitude of potential problems relating to production. The production manager is the direct supervisor for the prop master.

Set Department/Scene Shop

The set department works with the set (scenic) designer, building and installing every scenic element intended for each production. The prop master works closely with this department, coordinating use of the scene shop and helping to realize the environment of the set.

The technical director, or TD, is responsible for translating the set designs into working drawings, making sure the set is built, installed, operated, and struck from the stage perfectly and safely.

31

The TD and prop master are known to bounce ideas off one another, coordinate building and load-in schedules, and collaborate on certain building aspects of the design. In the past, the prop master reported to the TD. Nowadays, this relationship is changing throughout the theater world. The prop master is recognized as an official department head and is an excellent co-worker to the TD. Other members of the scene shop can include an assistant technical director, master carpenter, shop foreman, and carpenters.

The scenic artist applies texture to and paints all the scenic elements in accordance with the set design. The prop master can rely on the scenic artist for all sorts of help with color mixing and paint technique instruction. Scenic artists are usually very generous with their paint supplies as long as their tools are handled and maintained with respect.

Electrics Department

The electrics department maintains and operates all of the theatrical lighting and sound equipment in the theater and interprets the requests and designs of the lighting and sound designer. Some theaters have a separate sound department.

The master electrician works with the lighting and sound designers. This position organizes all the duties and schedules of the electrics department, including light hang and focus, sound equipment installation, and strike of both. The prop master relates information to the master electrician regarding any props that affect this department such as window treatments, lighting, and other electrified practical props. Other electrics personnel can include an assistant master electrician, electricians, light board operator, sound engineers, and sound board operator.

Costume Department/Costume Shop

The costume department recreates all of the costume designs created by the costume designer, making sure that each piece fits the appropriate actor perfectly. The prop master and the costume department share tools. (Well, mostly the prop master borrows the tools in the costume shop.)

The costume shop manager organizes actor fittings, manages costume shop staff, and works directly with the costume designer concerning the build of each costume piece. The costume shop manager and the prop master coordinate color and prop design decisions in collaboration with designers and guest artists to ensure that the look of the show comes together as it should. Typical topics of discussion include colors of props and costumes and costume prop needs. Other positions common to a costume department include an assistant costume shop manager, cutter/draper, stitchers, wardrobe supervisor, wig and makeup technician, and the costume running crew, or dressers.

Stage Management

The stage management department keeps the entire show organized and operating smoothly. This team of people is visible from well before rehearsals begin all the way through the strike of the show, handling a barrage of requests and demands for scheduling, information, organization, and time and energy. The prop master works with the entire crew to provide and organize prop needs for the show.

The stage manager has a role that is so broad it is hard to nail down. To simplify the job, this person provides the director with assistance during rehearsals and manages the backstage crew, actors, and all production operations during performances. The prop master relies on the stage manager for all prop changes or information generated during rehearsals and for repair notes from performances. Other stage manager team members include an assistant stage manager, journeyman, and stage/running crew.

Creative Guest Artists

Creative guest artists are exactly that — people who may or may not have full-time seasonal positions within the theater and therefore are the theater's guests during the time of their employment. Some theaters hire creative artists as full-time staff members to work on every production; other theaters opt to use the dramatic skills of their full-time staff only a few times during a season, providing an opportunity to see a variety of talent from many "outside" artists.

Director

The director is like the captain of a creative ship, steering and coordinating designers and production personnel toward the same theatrical concept for the show. If you know the ropes (no pun intended), the leadership of the director will help guide the work of the prop master safely into harbor.

Choreographer

Choreographers direct performers into stylized movement to enhance the storytelling of the play. Both fight and dance choreographers require specific props during their training.

Music Director

The music director works in collaboration with the director, yet is in charge of all the musical aspects of a production including teaching the actors their musical parts and rehearsing with and directing the musicians or orchestra. On rare occasions actors will play instruments, and the musical director and prop master will coordinate which instruments work the best.

Set Designer

The set designer works with the director to come up with the physical environment, or set, for the play. The prop master works directly with the set designer in providing props that are appropriate for the show and fit within the set design.

Light Designer

The light designer creates and models all of the lighting effects and chooses which instruments best suit the design. With approval from the scenic designer and director, lighting designers may ask the prop master to provide practical prop options that not only work with the set design, but also fit the light design needs for intensity and mood.

Costume Designer

The costume designer is responsible for enhancing the personality of the characters through the design of the costumes. Very often props will help define a character and are incorporated into the design of a costume. The costume designer and prop master work together to determine which props complete the costumes and work well for the actors.

Sound Designer

Sound designers create all the sound cues for the show. These people plan out speaker and microphone placement throughout the stage space according to what works best for the production. Some sound designers and directors prefer live sounds rather than recorded sound cues, which means that the prop master provides crash boxes, thunder sheets, door slam effects, etc., when needed.

Actors

Actors physically, mentally, and verbally portray the characters in the play. Actors will make requests for changes to current props or suggest new props during rehearsals. The prop master will discuss prop function with the actors, but most of the notes from the actors are passed on through the stage manager or director.

Educational Outreach

In response to increased interest in using the theater to serve niches of the community, most regional theaters have developed education departments. Much fun can be had between the prop master and the folks in the education departments. Prop requests often lead to stimulating creative discussion about how best to stage a show; these discussions often prove to be the starting point of a worthwhile venture down the road of the strange and creative.

Chapter 4
A Successful
Work Environment

"I wonder how this theater works."
Getting a sense on how your theater
really works is an important first step in
safeguarding against misunderstandings and
business mishaps. Protecting yourself by
knowing the ins and outs of your contract,
whether you are a freelance prop artisan or
a full-time employee, will help to set the
rules of your job within the company and
keep you from feeling taken for granted.

Have you ever been really excited about getting a job and realized once you started that it was nothing like you thought it was going to be? Maybe the job is going very well, but it's the inner workings of the theater that don't quite meet your expectations. Maybe the way the theater operates or the types of shows produced just don't mesh with you. Maybe this is the best place you have ever worked. Maybe you love your theater and your job so much that you never seem to have time to eat because you are so dedicated to the work.

No matter if you are job hunting or preparing for your fifth season, remember that the more you know about the theater you work for, the better off you will be. Seems like a simple statement, but many theater technicians jump right into the job without doing any research on the company ahead of time. Besides knowing that you'll be working as the prop master, find out what other expectations the theater has of you and what the perks of the job will be. Above all, know your limits, voice your needs, and protect yourself.

What Is Your Theater Like?

Type of Institution

What type of theater organization do you work with? Are you working in commercial, professional, community, college, or high school theater? The kind of organization in which you work will affect how you work. The propping processes will remain the same no matter what kind of theater organization you work with, but how these places conduct business can differ widely. For example, a professional theater is not going to have the same methods of operation and business structure as a school theatre would. Even though the aspects of putting the show together would be similar, the framework and chains of command vary and will have a bearing on how you accomplish your work. Institutional differences are expected. If you are new to a theater, be mindful of how your theater is set up and operates.

Venue and Stage

Every single theater space, or *venue*, is different. Does your theater utilize a cafetorium, a black box, an amphitheater, a church sanctuary, a gymnasium, or a concert hall? The *intimacy*, or the audience's proximity to the stage, plays a huge role in how detailed and realistic your props will be. What kind of stage is it — a proscenium, thrust, or arena? The type of stage influences the set design, which in turn has a huge effect on the props. A proscenium theater is a stage that looks like it is inset in a picture frame — the proscenium arch. The action takes place upstage of the arch, and the audience seating is downstage of the arch. A thrust stage invites the audience to sit on three sides of the stage. The fourth side is viewed as upstage. The audience is able to view the set at more angles. An arena stage is like a wrestling ring, without the ring, of course. The audience sits on all four sides of the stage. Props chosen to act on this kind of stage need to look nice on all sides and from all angles.

Work Space

Where is the prop shop located at your theater? Is it within the theater building, or is it *off-site*, located somewhere else in town? Do you have your own office and workspaces, or do you share space with the set department? The space in which you have to work has a huge impact on how you approach your projects and whose toes you might step on in the process. If your shop is within the theater building, the company may curb any work while a performance is happening. If your shop is off-site, travel time to and from the theater can really eat into your day.

Amenities

Are you allowed access into all areas of the theater, especially the workspaces of other production departments? Get the low down about what you're allowed to do within the theater building. What is the parking situation like at your theater? The prop master goes shopping a whole heck of a lot. When you are in and out of the car all day, constantly having to find places to park gets old fast. Maybe you can coerce someone to assign you your very own parking space.

Does the theater own a company vehicle, like a truck or van you can use regularly for shopping trips and hauling? Carting a vintage fridge on the roof of your car would be quite a feat (and funny to see). If the theater does not have its own cargo type of vehicle, then extra planning and creativity will be needed to figure out an alternative means of transportation.

What is located near the theater or prop shop? Knowing where to find the closest hardware, fabric, craft, and grocery stores will come in handy. Find out where the closest restaurants and watering holes are … for lunch meetings with the set designer, of course!

Security

Many theater buildings are strategically placed in downtown areas or on campuses, and off-site scene shops are usually pretty remote. Will you be safe working in the theater late at night? Ask your theater staff what safety precautions they recommend for their employees and what the neighborhood is like. Find out which keys access which rooms, how late you're allowed to stay in the building, and if the building has an alarm that needs to be armed when you are the last person to leave.

Storage Spaces

Do you have designated areas to store your props? You'll need to have at least a few places for storing set props, set dressing, and hand props. Hopefully these places can be easily accessed at any time. Not all storage spaces are ideal, yet most of them are accommodating enough. One theater I worked at stored props at a very creepy public storage facility with a bad history. Needless to say, the prop master refused to ever go there to pull props. Being afraid of prop storage is not a good thing, and concerns you have about the places you need to access most should be shared with your supervisor.

Your Theater's Policies and Procedures

Every theater will expect you to follow its procedures of operation, but most of these requests are never out of the ordinary. Most policies and procedures of an organization are instituted for practical business purposes. While you are answering the needs of the theater, have these same procedures work for you.

Budgets and Accounting

The financial practices and expectations of the prop master are fairly standard in the theater world. The prop department falls among the top three departments that spend the most money. All this spending produces receipts, which translates into lots of paperwork. Before you begin working, ask your supervisor and finance director to answer your important questions:

- How will I pay for prop purchases?
- Will I use cash and have a petty cash amount assigned to me, or will I have my own credit cards connected to theater accounts?
- What procedures does the theater want me to follow when I need to turn in receipts or be reimbursed?
- What are my prop budgets?
- Do I have budgets for show materials, labor, travel, resources, and prop shop supplies?
- Have I set up a good system for tracking my department's expenditures?
- What do I do with revenue brought in through rentals or sales of props?
- Can I have copies of all the necessary paperwork?
- Can I be reimbursed for mileage?

Taking good care of your budgets and financial paperwork will keep you in good standing with the financial department.

Renting Props to Others

When other companies, theaters, schools, or individuals borrow or rent props or tools from your department, it is wise to have the person responsible for the borrowing or renting fill out a rental agreement. The same applies when you borrow or rent items from other companies, theaters, schools, or individuals. The rental agreement serves many purposes and covers a great deal of ground between the person who is renting and the person who owns what is being rented.

The rental agreement primarily sets down the rules and terms of the deal. It will state if you are borrowing (using something for free) or renting (paying a fee to the renter). It is a record of who you are, where to find you, what you're borrowing, how long you intend to borrow it, and your promise to return it in the condition you borrowed it in (unless otherwise discussed and agreed to by borrower) by the date you specified, or you will pay the fines or fees as outlined in the agreement.

Both the owner and renter should sign and date the agreement and keep a copy for themselves. If you are borrowing something from someone who does not have a specific agreement, create one. The rental agreement not only protects the renter, but can keep the person renting out of hot water too. (See Chapter 6 for more rental agreement information.)

Communication and Schedules

A prop master is a great communicator, but she cannot share this skill if she does not have the proper tools. Will your theater assign you a work e-mail address connected to the organization? What is your office phone number and extension? Can you log into your email and check your phone messages remotely? Does the theater order business cards and name tags for new employees automatically, or will you need to supply them yourself? If you use your cell phone for work purposes, does the theater reimburse you for those calls?

The prop master's calendar will be full even before the job officially starts. Note when all theater activities fall in the calendar, including design meetings, staff meetings, production meetings, first rehearsal dates, meet and greet times, the beginning of tech week, dress rehearsal night, preview dates, and when the show opens. Your theater may hold special events and annual fundraisers that you may be expected to attend. Ask your boss how you can access the theater's master calendar and what programs or events will require your participation.

Protecting Yourself

Regardless of the setting in which you find yourself working, you need to protect yourself as a human being and as an employee/volunteer. Although physical safety is covered in Chapter 10, the human resource management side of prop mastering is another safeguard that should not be disregarded. Making sure that you are not burning the candle at both ends, being taken advantage of, or under-working yourself will greatly impact your happiness in your job.

Commitments vs. Contracts

Commitments

When you volunteer your time, you are committing yourself to the project at hand. Many prop masters volunteer their services to school and community groups or even to small professional theater companies that cannot afford to pay anything. Although rewarding, being a volunteer can have its down side. Volunteer prop masters encounter many inconsistencies in scheduling and communication that are vital for the completion of the prop list. Enter into any commitment with clearly defined expectations of your own. Be clear about your work hours and what deadlines you can realistically keep. Plan several work calls with other volunteers and seek out other dedicated people who are willing to help you. Being a volunteer prop master is an excellent way to share your talents with a great community of theater lovers.

Contracts

It is mostly in professional and commercial theater where you'll find paid prop masters. If you're getting paid — legally that is — then you've signed some form of a contract or letter of agreement. Most often, theaters choose to have their employees sign a letter of agreement. This letter lists the basics of the terms between employer and employee and isn't as confusing as most contracts. It omits many of the legal provisions commonly found in contracts. If not careful, the prop master may sign something that really means something else. If your letter of agreement does not specifically outline your job duties and express the theater's full range of expectations, you are taking a risk. Ask for a copy of the job description and employee handbook along with the letter. If the agreement does not look right, you can renegotiate and ask that the agreement be more detailed. Every letter of agreement or contract should state a rate of pay, the duration of employment, benefits (if applicable), and job duties. Figure 4.1 is a modified version of a common letter of agreement. You will get a sense of just how basic and vague this type of agreement really is.

Contracts or letters of agreement are signed by freelance prop artisans, seasonal prop masters, and full-time prop masters. Freelance artisans usually "float" through the theater community, working one show at a time and bouncing from one theater to the next. Many theaters do not employ full-time prop masters, counting on the availability of artisans in their areas. Seasonal prop masters are hired for work that is full time, yet only for a nine-month contract (similar to a school year). Many theaters that produce shows through the winter months go dark during the summer. Seasonal employees find themselves hunting for summer work before the winter months are half over.

LETTER OF AGREEMENT

(DATE)

This Agreement is agreed to by   Name of Employee   (hereinafter referred to as Employee) and   Name of Company   (hereinafter referred to as Theater.) Theater hereby hires Employee as Prop Master.

1.   **Term of Employment:** Employment shall commence on   (date)   , and shall continue through and include   (date).

2.   **Compensation:** Theater shall pay Employee the hourly rate of $_____ minus all taxes and deductions required by law, with payment made every Thursday during the duration of employment.

3.   **Benefits:** Employee shall receive (a) two (2) sick days per month of employment ; (b) two (2) weeks paid vacation. Medical and dental benefits as outlined in the Employee Handbook.

4.   **Job Duties:** Employee shall carry out the responsibilities as outlined in the Employee's job description (see Addendum A) and as determined by the Production Manager and Artistic Director.

5.   **Employee Handbook:** Employee has received, read and understands the information provided in the Employee Handbook.

6.   **Termination:** The Employee and the Theater have the right to terminate this Agreement at any time, providing the other party with two (2) weeks written notice. Theater also reserves the right to terminate the Agreement at any time with just cause as outlined in the Employee Handbook.

AGREED TO AS OF THE DATE FIRST STATED ABOVE:

_____	_____
Employee Signature	Theater Representative
_____	_____
Address	Job Title
_____	
City, State, Zip	
_____	
SS #	

Figure 4.1

Payment for Services

Always clarify before you begin working what your pay will be. This should be stated in your contract or letter of agreement. Your contract should include your rate of pay and when you will be paid — weekly, bi-weekly, or monthly. The pay period should also be stated clearly enough for you to know the date and frequency of your paychecks. If not stated in you contract, find out the method in which you will be paid — electronic deposit, check, or cash? Ask about tax deductions and fill out the correct state and federal paperwork before you start working. Some full-time employees are eligible for overtime pay and comp time. Find out if you will be compensated for working well beyond the hours of the normal work week.

Work Schedule

Confirm the Expected Work Schedule/Hours

Not everyone has the gumption when seeking employment or accepting a prop position to ask his boss or director what kind of work hours will be expected from the props department. Either prop masters don't think to ask about this, or they don't want employers or theater leaders to assume that they aren't willing to work hard. Just like any other job, it is your right to know what your supervisor expects of you. Your boss also has the right to learn of any major conflicts or engagements you may have that will affect your schedule. Having a forthright discussion about your work hours will ease the pressure and help you decide if you really have the time for this job.

The demands of theater require odd working hours. There is no getting around this. It is never a regular forty-hour-a-week type of business. There may be times when these regular hours can be found, but once tech week rolls around, you might as well just roll up your sleeves and accept the fact that you'll be putting in many extra hours. It is an understood rule of theater that the job must get done, that the show *must* go on! You have deadlines to meet per day, per project, per theater schedule. There is also a certain passion that circumvents those that work in theater. All of us who work or dabble in prop mastery do our work for the love of the art — "For the the-uh-tah!" We work hard because we love the challenge and the payoff. Despite the atmospheric "hurrahs," gratitude, and astounding sense of accomplishment, most prop masters hit opening night celebrations with sore muscles, dragging feet, and toothpicks propping open eyelids. We're exhausted.

Propping a show is time consuming, and most prop masters push themselves to find or build the perfect prop even if that means starting the day early and staying up late. We prop in between classes, sneak in prop hunting calls during our work breaks, or spend our entire day sans meals searching for the silver-plated samovar because nothing else is quite right. We never seem to stop and take time for ourselves even though we want to very badly.

Before you get to the point where you may dash away from a production meeting in tears of exhaustion, stop and breathe. No good prop master wants to compromise the integrity of his work or work ethic. Working so much that you exhaust your energy and creativity and have no time for play is compromising yourself. Every prop master wants to have his show completed and nicely done, but a fine balance can be found so neither the show nor yourself has to suffer.

Communicate Your Needs

Look at your lists and look at your time. Compare the two. Do you have enough time in your day to meet the demands of rehearsals? Do you have enough time each week to sufficiently chisel away at your prop lists? Will you have enough time between now and the start of technical rehearsals to supply the suitable props for the show? Be honest: if you suspect the show may suffer because of your time vs. workload, ask to speak to your leader, director, or boss about the situation. If you calmly express your concern in advance, your leaders may be able to find alternative ways of helping you achieve your propping goals.

Take Care of Yourself

1. Sleep. Your body and your mind need sleep. This is a proven medical fact. I am not suggesting you languish in bed for most of the day and miss an entire technical rehearsal. I *am* suggesting that you get an appropriate amount of sleep per night so you may rise in the morning and face your next day refreshed.

2. Eat. Your body and mind need nutrients to keep you going during the day. This is another proven medical fact. If you skip your meals so that you can keep working and make a deadline, you most likely won't have enough energy to haul sofas to the rehearsal hall, let alone make it through the rest of the day. If you know your time is too crunched to step away from your work for any length of time, bring your lunch, clear a space for your food, and take at least fifteen minutes to sit and eat.

3. Know your daily limits. Whether you work as a professional, a student, or a volunteer prop master, you need to have a time in the day in which you stop working on props and focus on personal needs. However your day is organized, make sure you have time after propping to incorporate your obligations, even if it is to get some homework done, tuck the kids into bed, or do a load of laundry. We all know that prop work is fathomless; so, too, will be your chores if you don't mind them. Once again, I am not suggesting you miss dress rehearsal because you need to clean the fridge. I *am* suggesting that you know your daily energy limits and try not to completely overextend yourself.

Employee Handbook

If you are handed an employee handbook, read it! There is always interesting and helpful information regarding your theater's policies and procedures concerning certain freedoms you may have.

If your contract or letter of agreement states that you are given vacation time or personal/sick leave, be sure to take this time. When you work in theater, vacation time is a valuable gift that should be used, not wasted. Not many companies will let you carry over unused vacation time to the next contract or monetarily reimburse you for time not taken. Check the employee handbook for any rules pertaining to vacations and time off. Most likely there are dates when you will not be allowed to take time off. Theater policies of all kinds are outlined in the employee handbook. From sexual harassment and drug use to holidays the theater recognizes and opening night party rules, the handbook is your indication of what your theater discerns as important to the welfare of the organization.

Chapter 5
The Prop Shop

"What materials do I need to be able to do my job?" As a prop master you need space to work and tools to work with. Work spaces and storage areas will keep you organized and working more efficiently. The ideas and lists in this chapter will help you check off the important components of your inventories or help you build them up. Maintaining the organization of these areas will also help with inventory control.

The Dream

It is always a wish of the prop master to have the ideal space in which to work: a huge building, all to himself, that is separate but in close proximity to the theater building and stage. A building designed for the sole purpose of working on props; honeycombed with enormous workspaces including a large office, a material and supply room, a soft goods room, a paint and dye deck, a wood and metal shop, a craft room, and many large- to warehouse-sized storage spaces. Alas, very few prop masters ever experience a working wonderland of this magnitude.

Touring other prop masters' prop shops is always interesting. Size, layout, and approximation to the stage will vary from one place to the next. Despite the cramped or spacious places in which prop masters usually find themselves working, the projects do get done. Typically, most prop masters have three spaces they maintain: an office, a workshop, and a storage space.

The Office

As a student prop master, I carried all my show information in my backpack, borrowed phones in the administration office to make calls, and jotted lists while sitting in a quiet corner of a hallway or student union. I wished for an office or desk of my own — a place where I could spread out and focus on my tasks. Back then, computers were not a standard office item or the necessity they are

46

now, so I can't rightfully complain that I "didn't even have a computer!" The reality is that not all prop masters have the luxury of an office equipped with the modern conveniences and the latest technology. Your "office" might be your dining room table, a makeshift table in a small corner of a dusty scene shop, or a furnished office convenient in every way. No matter what is determined as your office, you need a space to sit down, make lists, study and fill out paperwork, use the phone, check e-mail, store your resources, focus, and regroup.

Not all theaters have the funds to supply their departments with the latest and greatest, yet most theaters do their utmost to provide quality, functioning workspaces for their prop departments. However, there is always wiggle room for improving upon what spaces are granted to your department. Don't hesitate to speak up if you have ideas that could improve your work environment. Theater supervisors may not be aware of your secret improvement desires. Once you become proactive and vocal about the things you need, you'll be surprised at how fast you start to obtain them.

When furnishing the ideal office of the prop master, start with the basics. To have a functioning office, you need a desk, and you need a chair. Obviously, you can choose what you'd prefer to have as your desk. You are not married to the metal desk with the thin pencil drawer above your lap. In actuality, you may not spend a lot of time at  your desk. Shopping, building, attending meetings, and all the running around you'll do will hinder your chances at grabbing a nap at your desk. However, much of your preliminary propping work will require a desk.

Other typical office furnishings that prop masters access daily are filing cabinets, bookcases, corkboards, and dry erase boards. Your resource books, information collections, and paperwork need organized housing of their own within your office.

Instruments of technology — computers and other office equipment — are standard accessories that are expected to be found in every office, and the prop office is no exception. Unfortunately, there are still theater prop offices that do not have these standard, albeit costly, machines. Prop masters utilize these machines daily. E-mails are sent, phone conversations are conducted, computer-designed props are printed in-house, budget spreadsheets are maintained, and antique telegrams are scanned or copied. The argument that the prop master is entitled to and required to have permanent access to basic (and advanced) office equipment is endless.

The fundamental list of office equipment:
• Modern computer with internet access
• All-in-one printer, copier, scanner
• Phone with answering machine
• Software for word processing, spreadsheets, photo altering

Office Supplies Shopping List

3-Ring binders
3-Hole punch
Calculator
Calendars
Clipboard
Envelope
File folders
Laminating sheets
Legal notepads
Paper clips
Paper cutter
Pens and pencils
Printing paper
Push pins
Rubber bands
Scissors
Sheet protectors
Standard ruler
Stapler
Steno notepads
Sticky notes
Tape dispenser

The prop office is not complete without office supplies, of course. Usually prop shop office supplies become prop-building supplies before they even have the chance of settling in as office or desk accessories. If you are setting up a new prop office, a trip to the office supply store is in order. A copy of the shopping list provided will help get you started.

The Workshop

If one didn't know any better, one could walk into the prop workshop and assume the prop master and artists were pirates, raiding goods from other theater production departments to pad the prop shop coffers (which is not to say this might not accidentally happen from time to time). The stock of materials and tools in the prop shop is extremely diverse, reflecting the peculiar and multifarious tasks relegated to this particular production department.

Of course, when you have a large amount of stuff, you need a way to organize it. Prop materials, supplies, tools, and building odds

Protection!

Before we go any further, the health and safety of you and your co-workers is of the utmost importance! Protecting yourself is a vital part of your work and should not be viewed as an optional convenience. The tools and materials you will work with on a daily basis can be hazardous. Take charge of your work environment and make it as risk free as possible. Tips on how to create a safer work environment and a detailed list of gear and supplies which aid in protecting your health are discussed in detail in Chapter 10.

and ends take up a lot of workshop space. Without a system of organization, you will be spending unnecessary amounts of time constantly sorting and searching. Allocate spaces, drawers, shelves, cubbies, and areas in the workshop to store your materials and supplies.

As you organize, keep similar things grouped together and organize your supplies and materials throughout the workshop in a manner that will be the most convenient and the most functional to you and your team. This may be a very obvious concept, but not all of us talented prop masters possess strong or even mediocre organizational skills. At some point during production, your prop shop will look like a tornado hit and swirled your materials and tools into a funky salad. (FYI: Board members and donors tend to always tour the theater and shops when the prop shop is looking its worst, never when it's nicely organized.) Yet, if you have an organizational system in place, finding the materials you need and cleaning up your messes will be a breeze.

With an enormous commercial industry focused on helping you with your every organizational and storage need, you should not have a problem amassing storage bins and shelving for your workshop. If you need to, hold a prop shop garage sale where the proceeds go toward buying storage bins. Besides meeting your propping deadline, nothing is more important than having a functional place in which to work.

Proper storage for hazardous supplies and materials ultimately makes for a happier work environment. Most state and local fire codes require chemicals and flammables to be stored in a specific kind of cabinet — The Safety Cabinet. These cabinets come in different sizes, are lockable, are made of metal, and are specially designed to meet federal OSHA requirements. They help prevent the risk of fire and segregate chemical vapors from common areas where people breathe. They are an excellent investment.

While you're considering it all — safety cabinets, storage cabinets, wall organizers, shelving, and where you'll eventually stash all of those materials and tools — remember to save space for work tables. Tables at desk- or dining table-height are perfect for sewing projects and detailed crafts. Standard prop shop work tables are thirty-six inches tall and at least four feet wide by eight feet long. You can make your own work table to the size that suits you best. Suitable chairs and stools and a few anti-fatigue floor mats will keep everyone in the prop shop going strong for a long time.

Every prop master will set up and organize his prop spaces differently. What works or makes sense to one person may seem like a complete mess to the next. Don't feel obligated to stick with a previously created workshop if you find that the scheme and arrangement does not work well with how you and your team would prefer things to be. No need to complain about how it was organized previously. No need to feel bad about wanting to reorganize it. Just change it. Take charge of your workspace.

Shop Supplies, Materials, and Parts

The prop shop is an amazing conglomeration of cleaning products, raw materials, hardware, and supplies. Every prop shop needs an organized stock of building and crafting odds and ends — stuff to make stuff with. Initially, prop masters start their collections out of a need for particular things. Eventually, these things turn into a nice healthy stock of an assortment of supplies, materials, and parts. Unless you begin to run out of space, there is no such thing as "too much stuff." A workshop full of odds and ends will always come in handy.

This section offers a taste of the different kinds of supplies, materials, and parts you would find in a typical prop shop and why this stuff is needed. If you are just starting out and in charge of gathering a basic inventory for your shop, you may find the shopping lists helpful. Highlighting some of the common and easy-to-find products and supplies used in propping, these lists are only a beginner's sampling of items prop masters work with over the course of a fiscal year.

Adhesives and Tapes

The joke that you cannot be an official prop master without owning a hot glue gun is true ... to a degree. However, a variety of adhesives and tapes makes life in the prop shop a heck of a lot easier. As you may well know, not all adhesives are equal. Adhesives are designed to work with specific materials and offer varying bonding strengths. Some adhesives may even dissolve the materials they are applied to, so it behooves you to research which adhesives serve your purposes best. The bond between surfaces once an adhesive is applied can be practically irreversible, so be aware of drips and what surfaces will be affected. You do not want to glue yourself to your project. More information regarding proper use of adhesives and health protection when using them can be found in Chapter 10.

Adhesives and Tapes Shopping List

Epoxy	Construction adhesive
Hot glue	Spray adhesive
Super glue	Rubber cement
White glue	Wood glue
Floral tape	Gaffers tape
Masking tape	Mortite
Packaging tape	Scotch® tape
Spike tape	

Cleaning Supplies

Cleaning supplies aren't just for swabbing down the shop bathroom or cleaning up spilled coffee. Sure, you'll eventually want to clean up the prop shop, especially after a series of messy projects, but these supplies are mainly for getting performance props ready. Props get dusty sitting in storage, materials you pull from the junk yard need a good sterilizing, and tea towels used in previous shows will start to mold. The props actors use for eating or drinking and props that carry food need to be washed. Before any props make their way into the rehearsal hall and into the hands of the actors, set aside some scrubbing time.

Cleaning Supplies Shopping List

All-purpose cleaner	Bleach
Carpet cleaner	Dish soap
Dustpan	Fabric detergent
Floor broom	Glass cleaner
Goof Off Remover	Goo Gone®
Lime Away	Lysol®
Magic Eraser	Paper towels
Push broom	Rags
Simple Green	Sponges
Spray bottles	

Polishing Supplies

Before you become discouraged with the thought that you'll have to refinish the dull wooden furniture in your show, try polishing first. Read the product directions before you polish; some polishes allow you to use steel wool and others require a non-abrasive cloth.

When polishing wood, always polish in the direction of the grain. Silver tends to need polishing every time you turn around, requiring polish more often than pewter, brass, or stainless steel. With a soft cloth, dry metal immediately after polishing to keep from having to repeat the process.

Polishing Supplies Shopping List

Furniture polish	Brass polish
Non-abrasive cloth	Old English®
Rags	Restor-a-Finish
Silver polish	Stainless steel polish
Steel wool	

The shopping lists found on pages 51-55 reflect products, supplies, and materials that will give you a jump start on filling your workshop with handy stuff. Think of your workshop as a miniature version of art supply, hardware, and fabric stores, with a mixture of your grandpa's basement, a cup of an electrician's van, a teaspoon of your fourth grade art teacher's classroom, and a dash of the corner parts and junk store.

Even though these shopping lists will get you started, or maybe give you a new product idea, they are not complete. There are just so many materials and supplies available in the world that it would take an entire book to discuss them all. Every prop master props differently and develops his own prop-building material and supply likes and dislikes. Some like to recreate a marble bust using modeling clay, others prefer to carve the bust out of foam, and there is always that one guy who will pull the block of marble out from under his desk and get to work.

Despite these preferences, there are handy materials that are common to the trade and fall under these categories:
• Art and craft supplies
• Casting and sculpting supplies
• Drawing supplies
• Foam supplies
• Hardware supplies
• Paper supplies
• Paint, stain, and miscellaneous supplies
• Wood supplies

Arts and Crafts Supplies

Beads	Buttons
Cotton balls	Embossing kits
Glitter	Laminating kits
Popsicle sticks	Wooden pieces

Drawing Supplies

Artist markers	Calligraphy kit
Charcoal	Colored pencils
Compass	Crayons
Paint pens	Pencils
Protractor	Rulers
Stencils	Permanent markers

Casting/Sculpting Supplies

Cans and containers	Casting resin
Chicken wire	Fiberglass
Model Magic®	Paperclay®
Papier-Mâché	Super Sculpey®
Rigid Wrap®	Wire Mesh

Foam Supplies

Floral foam	Insulating foam
Pink insulating panels	Polystyrene (Styrofoam)
Spray insulating foam	Upholstery foam
Sculpt or Coat®	Foam Coat™

Paper Supplies

Brown craft paper	Butcher paper
Construction paper	Drawing paper
Graphite transfer paper	Illustration board
Mat board	Newsprint
Photo paper	Poster board
Tracing paper	

Paints, Stains, Misc. Supplies

Acrylic	Clear coat spray (gloss & matte)
Denatured alcohol	Dulling spray
Fabric dye	Flame retardant
Floral spray	Glass paint
Latex paint	Mild dish soap
Mineral spirits	Mod Podge®
Murphy's Oil Soap®	Plastic varnish
Scenic paint	Spray paint
Stain	Starch
Stripper	Transparent Wood Tones

Wood and Accoutrement Supplies

1 x 4" pine	2 x 4" pine
Joint compound	Luan
Masonite	MDF
Plywood	Putty
Sandpaper	Wooden dowels

Hardware Supplies

Hooks and hangers	Wire
Plumber's tape	Casters
Furniture glides	Nails and screws
Nuts and bolts	Washers
Chain	Clothesline
Jute	Tie line
Zip cord	Metal and plastic pipe
Plexiglas	Tubing

Shop Tools

Shop tools are the instruments in your workshop or in the general scene shop that make it possible to build or modify props. Every workshop should possess the very basic tools. The basics are the necessary tools that keep your shop in operation. Having more tools than those listed below can only benefit the quality of your work and simplify your life. Big jobs cannot be done with small tools and vice versa. Tool size and strength vary depending on what types of jobs they were built to do.

Hand Tools

Hand tools are construction instruments requiring no electrical or battery-operated power, just physical human strength and guidance.

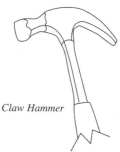

Claw Hammer

Hammers

Hammers come in a variety of shapes and sizes. Only one type of hammer, the *claw hammer*, is used for nailing and pulling out nails. For upholstery work, the *tack hammer* is specially designed to be lightweight and

Rubber mallet

have a smaller head for attaching different kinds of upholstery tacks. A *rubber mallet* won't leave the marks a metal hammer does when needing to fit together or knock apart delicate surfaces.

Hand Saws

The *crosscut saw* is what most people picture when they think of a hand saw. It is fairly long and cuts across the grain of the wood. More teeth per inch on the saw blade results in a smoother cut. The *hacksaw* is perfect for cutting metal dowels and other soft or mild strength metals.

Crosscut saw   *Hacksaw*

Measuring and Framing Tools

Why spend your time building something if it won't be the right size in the end? Tape measures, yardsticks, rulers, an architect's triangular scale, framing squares, quick squares, a box level, and chalk lines were invented particularly because of the need to

Chalk line

make something a certain size and shape. Without these tools, edges would not be straight, legs could be different lengths, and, well, no one would be happy.

Tape measures are long, retractable metal strips coiled inside a plastic or metal case. The metal strips have markings like a ruler and can extend to reach fifty feet or more. *Yardsticks* and *rulers* are common household items which aid in drawing and measuring straight lines. An *architect's triangular scale* is a ruler and measuring tape of sorts. Its actual job is to make drawings or take measurements from "scale drawings" (ground plans and elevations) of different ratios. For example, if a ground plan is drawn in half-inch scale, this means that every half-inch on the drawing equals one foot in real life. The triangular scale is triangular in shape; each side is designed to accommodate the many ratios used in varying scale drawings.

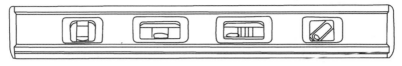

Box level

Framing squares and *speed squares* check the ninety-degree accuracy of corners. The framing square is steel, L-shaped, and can also act as a ruler with the long side measuring inches up to two feet and the short side showing about sixteen inches in length. The speed square looks like a right triangle complete with hypotenuse, and is also designed to aid with the creation of other angles.

A *box level*, or carpenter's level, is a straight metal frame lined with bubble vials that determine if a horizontal line is level or a vertical line is plumb. A *chalk line* draws long lines wherever you may need them. The line is actually a string wound in a metal case, saturated with colored chalk. When the string is pulled from the case, stretched tight at two opposing points, and snapped, the chalk will leave a visible, straight line across the project.

Paintbrushes and Supplies

Prop masters paint often. I have ruined many pairs of jeans and shirts because I would head off to work ill-prepared and wind up painting. After several pairs of painter's pants were "created," I learned to keep a set of painting clothes on hand at work. If you are painting at work and need paint clothes, you will obviously need the tools for this particular job as well.

Brushes: Prop masters need two selections of brushes; the "good" brushes and the "disposable" brushes. The good brushes should consist of detail brushes of various sizes (for small craft projects and fine art painting), a graining brush (for wood grain techniques), a couple of nice lay-in brushes (flat brushes for the purpose of "laying down" the paint on a surface), sash brushes in different widths (angled brushes for cutting in against hard lines), a foliage brush (essentially a large-scale detail brush), and a stipple brush (so as not to ruin your other brushes when dabbing paint through a stencil). Disposable brushes can be used for adhesives, stains, shellac, and homemade textures. Chip and foam brushes are inexpensive and come in one- to four-inch widths.

Paintbrush care

Paint should never be allowed to dry on a brush, and brushes should be cleaned immediately after use. When cleaning immediately is not an option, soak your brushes in a bucket of warm water until you have time to attend to them, but do not leave them to soak overnight. Many scenic artists like to use Murphy's Oil Soap® when cleaning natural bristle brushes because it won't strip the oil out of the bristles like common soaps will. A wire brush is a handy tool when paint is too stubborn to wash out. Be sure to comb out the paint in the direction of the bristles. Brushes should be washed until the water runs clear. If oil paints were used, quickly dipping or gently swishing the brush into a shallow bucket of mineral spirits will help release the paint from the bristles; then clean as normal.

Sprayers: Are just as important to a scenic artist as his brushes and just as handy for a prop master. Sprayers use a watery paint mixture to add texture and visual dimension to props, drops, and other scenery. *Garden sprayers* are great for spraying varying sized droplets of paint over large areas with hand pumped, pressurized air. *Pneumatic sprayers* have a more refined and consistent spray because these sprayers hook into the compressed air system of the scene shop. *Aerosol sprayers* act like cans of spray paint and are great for toning and distressing props and large-scale detail work.

Sprayer care

Place a funnel covered with a nylon paint strainer into the opening of the sprayer container and strain your paint as you pour it from the bucket to avoid objects from plugging the mechanics of the sprayer. Clean the sprayer immediately after use. Release or disconnect the pressurized air from the sprayer and remove the container. Rinse the container and refill it with warm clear water, then reassemble the container to the mechanism. Operate the sprayer turned towards a sink until the nozzle sprays clear water. Release, disconnect, and remove once more and set the parts out to dry. If you fail to clean your sprayer, paint will dry in the tubing and nozzles rendering it nearly useless.

Rollers and Sponges: Gather roller frames, roller covers, a roller pan, and plastic liners, and you are set for applying a thick, even coat of paint on your project. Rollers and accessories are located at any mega retail or hardware store and are reusable. Sponges are also readily available. Natural and synthetic sponges create interesting paint textures and grains and softly blend paints together.

Roller care

Rinse roller cover under water when using water-based paint. The cover is just as porous as a sponge and will take some time to completely clean. Squeeze excess water from cover and set upright to dry. If the roller covers are not cleaned, the paint will harden making them unusable. If you bought pan liners, any remaining paint can be poured back into the paint can and the liner can be thrown away. Otherwise, the paint pan will also need a hardy rinse. Sponges need to be rinsed until the water runs clear and given a thorough squeeze before setting out to dry.

Painting tools: A healthy supply of painting accessories in the prop shop will be a great gift to yourself when it is time to paint:

• Paint Stirrers — the ingredients in paint separate when paint sits for any length of time; paint either needs to be stirred or remixed before being applied to your project.

• Paint Key — a can opener designed specifically for prying open paint can lids. In a pinch, a slotted screwdriver would fit the bill.

• Drop Cloths — these could be store bought or a found piece of material. An old, unusable drop, yards of old fabric, plastic tarps, craft paper, and newspaper provide excellent drop cloth protection.

• Masking Tape — less expensive than the traditional blue painters tape, yet does the same job and comes in many widths. Use this tape to mask off parts of your project that need not be painted.

• Buckets — quart cans and one-gallon and five-gallon buckets can be purchased at hardware stores or recycled from finished supplies. You never know what you'll need a bucket for: watering down white glue, mixing new paint colors, soaking linens in bleach, or transporting small props or tools.

Pliers

Pliers are invaluable because of their "strength" when gripping things. Almost like having a strong replacement hand, pliers hold things in place, bend and twist metal, and grab hold of tiny parts. *Slip-joint pliers* are the most basic and can be adjusted at the joint of the jaws depending on the width of the object. *Needle-nose pliers* have long and thin jaws used for gripping small objects. *Wire cutters* fall under the pliers family, yet they are used to cut small-gauge wire.

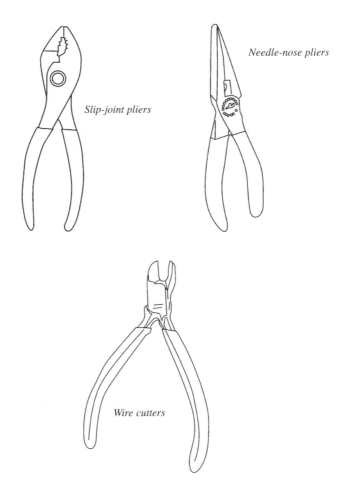

Needle-nose pliers

Slip-joint pliers

Wire cutters

Screwdrivers

Screwdrivers tighten and remove screws and come in sets that offer a variety of widths and lengths. Avoid buying inexpensive screwdrivers that only offer plastic blades or tips. The plastic will break at the slightest bit of pressure and at the most inopportune time. The two types of standard screwdriver sets you should initially seek are *Slotted* and *Phillips* head. Slotted screwdrivers have flat blades of varying thicknesses and widths made to fit flat or rounded head slotted screws. Phillips screwdrivers have a cross-like tip designed to exert more force when driving in flat or rounded Phillips-head screws

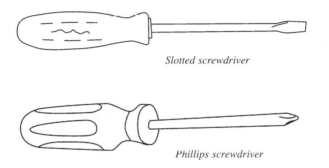

Slotted screwdriver

Phillips screwdriver

Wrenches

Wrenches tighten nuts and bolts. Having a variety of wrenches is a great gift. If you had to choose just one, then the *crescent wrench*, or adjustable-end wrench, is the one to pick. The crescent wrench adjusts to grip standard-sized theater bolt head and nuts, fits nicely in your back pocket, and is the most sought-after wrench for all technical theater staff. A set of *Allen wrenches*, or hex keys, helps with putting together the "easy to assemble" furniture of today, as these fit into and tighten those darn cap screws.

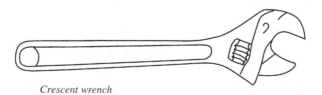

Crescent wrench

Miscellaneous Tools

A tool no prop master can live without is a *staple gun*. The staple gun will assist in upholstery crafts and other building projects and will quickly tack rugs to the stage floor and tablecloths to café tables to prevent potential disasters.

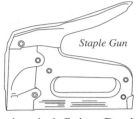

Staple Gun

A staple gun's problem-solving uses are rather indefinite. Don't prop without one.

More Handy Tools To Have Eventually

Ball peen hammer
Bolt cutter
C-clamps
Chisel set
Conduit bender
Coping saw
Crowbar
End nippers
Engraving tools
File
Flash cut saw
Forstner bits
Grommet punch
Hole saw
Keyhole saw
Laminating machine
Locking pliers
Nut driver set
Open-end wrench set
Pipe cutter
Rasp
Ratchet and socket set
Staple puller
Table vise
Tweezers
Wire stripper

A *mat knife* is another must-have because it cuts through carpet, cardboard boxes, etc. *X-acto® knives* create small precision cuts, perfect for small craft or model making. Another item, the *putty knife*, is not a knife but more of a spatula for smearing joint compound, putty, and other pudding-like materials onto projects. *Scissors* are a precious tool that require no explanation.

Inadvertent strength training is a guarantee for the prop master, but pulling a muscle (or worse) can be prevented by using *furniture dollies* and *hand trucks* to assist with moving large props from one place to another.

Power Tools

A power tool is any tool that is electrically or battery powered. Some tools are a bit more powerful than others. All the human has to do is guide or monitor the tool while it is operating; barely any muscle power required. However, despite the degree of power a power tool takes or shells out, all of them are dangerous. (Power tool safety is discussed in Chapter 10.)

Tool Accessories

Most tools have some part that is either replaceable or interchangeable, or just needs a special accessory that is convenient for completing the task.

Examples:
* Disposable Batteries
* Drill bit sets
* Extension cords
* Ironing boards
* Rechargeable batteries
* Sandpaper
* Saw blades (metal and wood)
* Screw tips

Soldering iron

Tools That Require Power

These items may not always appear to be very powerful, but are still tools that need to be plugged in.

Electric Knife: Designed to slice through turkey and breads, this knife dubs as the perfect cutter for upholstery foam and is a fantastic carving tool.

Fans: Not only perfect for ventilation needs, but will also dry glue and paint in half the time. Box fans and industrial oscillating fans are usually preferred.

Hot Glue Gun: A staple tool of the prop master. This tool heats up solid glue sticks to a very hot honey consistency that can adhere just about anything.

Hot Knife: A tool that uses heat to cut through Styrofoam and pink foam insulation for carving and crafting.

Hot Plate: Like a miniature stove top with up to two burners. Can be plugged into a wall socket. Used to heat pots of water or soup for lunch — whatever is necessary.

Soldering Iron: For projects that require thin metals or wires to bond permanently, soldering promises a better hold than anything else. The iron heats and melts the solder which can then be applied to the metal surfaces. Flux is used to clean these surfaces beforehand to ensure a better bond.

Slightly More Powerful Tools

This bare bones list of power tools could help the prop shop "get by" in a pinch.

Hand Sander: A rather luxurious time saver. Using vibration and sandpaper, the hand sander can smooth rough edges or strip paint off a chest of drawers in less time it takes to bake a cake.

Jig Saw: Also known as a saber saw. A hand-held tool with a reciprocating blade used to cut curved patterns in wood (mostly sheet goods) and plastics.

Screw gun

Screw Gun: (Or cordless drill, as so many properly call it.) Second only to the hot glue gun for assembling (and disassembling) props. This power tool has a variable-speed motor controlled with a finger trigger and delivers a high amount of torque. The drill bits and screw tips are interchangeable, and the tool is supplied with a rechargeable battery.

Wet/Dry Vacuum: Also known as a shop vac, a prop and scene shop staple. More than just your everyday vacuum, this machine won't complain or fall apart when reporting for heavy duty. The body of the vacuum is a huge collection chamber on wheels that can be emptied directly. The inside filter can be removed when dealing with liquid messes, and the long plastic hose is easy to clean and comes with different vacuum attachments.

Powerful Power Tools

Husky power tools will always be needed (or wanted), and hopefully you will have access to the theater's scene shop, which will have a better selection of larger and stronger tools for larger, heftier projects. Most prop shop workspaces are too small to accommodate the space needed for these larger power tools. What these wonderful tools are and how they can ease your building process and progress are detailed below. (Please do not rely on this information as instructions for operation.)

Band Saw: Presents the ability to cut irregular shapes of wood or metal. The saw blade is actually a band of metal that rides on two wheels inside a metal case. The width of the band determines how tight a curved cut can be made.

Bench Grinder: A medium-sized stationary motor with two rotating shafts on either side equipped with various wheels with which to grind, polish, and buff metal or plastics.

Bench Sander: A medium-sized stationary tool with a revolving flat belt of sandpaper to smooth edges on plastic and wood.

Drill Press: Mounted to either a stand or bench and used to drill precise holes in wood or metal. It can handle heavy-duty projects and use larger diameter drill bits than an electric or battery-operated drill.

Dry Cut Metal Saw: Similar in look to a miter saw, yet can hold lengths of metal, tubing, and pipe in place while making an accurate cut.

Lathe: Used most often to create turned wooden legs for furniture, newel posts, spindles, etc. The lathe spins a block of wood at a fast rate. When the controlled application of tools is pressed against the spinning block of wood, cuts of various curves and depths can be made.

Miter Saw: A machine commonly used for trim and molding cuts, but can crosscut pieces at an accurate ninety-degree angle or pivot to make angled miter cuts. These machines can be built to tilt and create compound angled cuts.

Panel Saw: An ideal one-person saw that is easy and safe to use. Like the table saw, the panel saw can rip large sheets of wood into strips. It can also make cross cuts with the blade facing away from the operator and towards the back of the machine.

Pneumatic Tools: Pneumatic staplers or nailers, for example, are similar to electric tools, except that they are powered by air pressure and therefore a lot more powerful. In order to operate pneumatic tools, the shop must have an air compressor and lines that will evenly distribute the air to handy area tool hook-ups within the space.

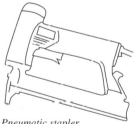

Pneumatic stapler

Radial Arm Saw: A vertical, circular blade secured in a yoke which slides back and forth along a horizontal arm positioned at a certain distance above the cutting plane. It is great for cross cutting long pieces of wood into more manageable or desirable sizes.

Reciprocating Saw: Nicknamed Sawzall because it saws just about everything, this sturdy, multi-cutting machine just needs the appropriate blade to cut through metal and wood. Great for strike and reducing a sofa to stackable bits.

Router: Uses specially made bits to decoratively carve or shape the edges or surfaces of tables, signs, molding, etc.

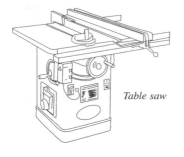

Table saw

Table Saw: Looks like a funky table with a circular saw. One of the more dangerous saws because of the open blade and kick-back issues, the table saw is invaluable for its ability to cut long lengths of wood into smaller widths with a straight and smooth edge. Wood is laid along the table of the machine horizontally.

Welder: A machine that fuses two metals together to create an extremely strong bond. Welders melt the metals, insert an added filler material to produce a molten puddle, and with pressure and heat can manipulate the puddles into beads, which, when cool, provide a durable marriage of material.

Basic Tool Care

Machines and tools wear out faster when they are not properly cared for. Quite honestly, no one person or business can afford to have disposable power tools — they are just too expensive! If you use the tool, regardless of who owns it, the responsibility of keeping it in working order falls on your shoulders. Simple and basic things you can do with maintaining these machines will give them long, powerful life spans.

- Unplug power cords from the wall while holding onto the plug, not while tugging on the cord.
- Brush sawdust, dirt, foam dust, and lint off machines when through working.
- Coil and tie the power cords of hand-held tools into nice bundles when not in use.
- Store hand-held power tools on designated shelves or in bins to keep them out of harm's way.
- Lubricate bearings and other movable parts that need this kind of maintenance on a regular basis. Make it your business to know what machines need this attention.
- Replace drill bits and saw blades for hand-held power tools and blades for the band saw and metal saw when they show signs of age.

- Regularly sharpen saw blades for larger saws such as the table and panel saws, radial arm, and miter saws.
- Clean saw blades often. Resin and other gunk builds up fast.
- At least once a year or when needed, service your machines. Saws, especially, can lose their alignment over time. A machine that is off-kilter will end up wearing out quickly and throw off the proper wear and tear of the blades which may affect the accuracy of your cuts.

Sewing Tools and Notions

Soft-good construction takes up a good amount of a prop master's build time. From crafting an intricate leather coin purse to very grand, very long curtains with swag valences, a prop master needs the sewing tools required to accomplish these tasks.

Sewing "Power" Tools

Many theaters cannot afford to double up on these machines; therefore, the prop and costume shops should always get along. Ideally, though, the prop shop would have these machines to call its very own.

Fabric Steamer: An easy tool to use to get the wrinkles out of curtains and tablecloths once they are installed on-stage. The base is a water container with a heating element inside that turns the water into steam after only a few short minutes. The steam is controlled through the nozzle and hose.

Irons: The basic iron is the everyday household iron. In the prop shop, this iron is best for use when attaching interfacing and iron-on patches to materials. An industrial iron can withstand being on for hours at a time. This type of iron is best when needing to iron large amounts of different types of fabrics.

Sewing Machine: A portable, heavy-duty sewing machine that can handle stitching multiple layers of thick fabrics is an ideal tool for the prop shop. Industrial sewing machines are designed to fit this bill, yet they are not portable and sometimes are too

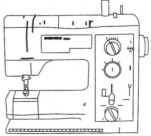

Sewing machine

"macho" to sew fine silk or offer a variety of interesting stitches. The sewing machine needs regular servicing, especially after heavy use. Stores that retail and repair sewing machines usually offer tutorials on care and maintenance of your machine.

Serger: Also known as an overlock, it's a heavy-duty machine that truly can kill two birds with one stone. In nearly one fell swoop, a seam is stitched together, a blade trims excess material a quarter inch from the seam, and needles make an overcast stitch over the freshly hewn edge of fabrics just shy of the new seam. The end result is a nicely trimmed seam where the fabric is prevented from unraveling.

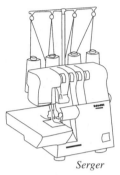

Serger

Washer/Dryer: Not only are these machines great for washing the starches and other gunk out of new materials and fabric props, a washer can double as a personal dye vat for larger dyeing and distressing jobs such as curtains, upholstery materials, and bed linens.

Sewing Notions: Hand Tools

Many sewing tasks are done by hand. This simple checklist offers the chance for soft-good perfection with fewer tears.

Clear plastic tailor rulers	Cloth measuring tape
Embroidery hoops	Hand sewing needles
Marking tools	Pinking shears
Scissors	Seam ripper
Standing hem marker	Tracing wheel
Upholstery needles	

Sewing Notions: Supplies

There are always those little odds and ends that you find you need for nearly every project but always wind up borrowing from the costume shop. Go ahead, splurge a little, and start accumulating a healthy stock for the prop shop:

Elastic	Machine needles
Straight pins	Safety pins
Snaps	Threads
Velcro	

Common Prop Shop Fabrics and Materials

As you continue propping, the many weaves and styles of fabrics and soft-good building materials will be as familiar to you as breathing. A little studying to impress your designers and directors never hurt either. Here are some very common fabrics and materials prop masters work with regularly.

Prop Shop Fabrics:

Brocade	Burlap	Calico
Canvas	Cheesecloth	Chenille
Chiffon	China silk	Chintz
Commando cloth	Crushed velvet	Duck cloth
Duvetyn	Erosion cloth	Felt
Gingham	Georgette	Lace
Leather	Lining	Muslin
Organza	Plether	Satin
Scrim	Silk	Spandex
Terrycloth	Ticking	Tissue Lamé
Tulle	Velour	Velvet
Vinyl	Wool	

Soft-Good Materials:

Batting	Interfacing	Pillow forms
Polyester filling	Rug liner	Upholstery foam

Shared Spaces

I only know of a handful of prop shops that are completely self-contained and don't have to share space or tools with another department. The real reason most prop shops share space with other departments isn't because of lack of funds or space; it is because of the need for camaraderie with fellow coworkers. How else would you organize the after-work happy hour? (Yes, you are allowed to have a good time with the people you work with. Anyone who disagrees should be forced to sort screws.)

It is true. Most prop masters share work space with other departments. The scene shop is the department with which props is mostly commonly paired. The two shops use the same types of tools and seem to be the two messiest departments. Prop departments spend a fair amount of time taking space away from the costume

Tool Kit Supply List:

Acrylic paint (black, brown)	Allen wrenches
Architect's triangular scale	Chalk line
Chip brushes	Claw hammer
Cloth measuring tape	Coat hooks
Cotton string	Crescent wrench
Cup hooks	Elastic
Epoxy	Furniture glides
Gaff tape	Hand sewing needles
Hot glue gun	Hot glue sticks
Jute	Mallet
Mat knife	Masking tape
Mortite calking cord	Needle nose pliers
Paper towels	Pencils
Phillips-head screwdrivers	Permanent markers
Picture nails	Safety pins
Sandpaper	Seam rippers
Scissors	Screw gun
Screws	Slip joint pliers
Spray adhesives (small can)	Slotted screwdrivers
Staple gun	Staple gun staples
Straight pins	Super glue
Quick squares	Tack hammer
Tape measure	Thread (black and white)
Upholstery needles	Velcro
Vinyl gloves	Wire spool
Wire cutters	

In addition to the tool kit, I usually bring along a box or bucket filled with fabrics, materials, and supplies that are specific to the show and tools that won't fit inside the tool kit.

Tools will break, be misplaced, or be adopted by another department. As mentioned before, label all of your tools and materials, obviously indicating that these items belong to your department. Every so often, take inventory of your tool kit and spend some time researching where any long-lost items might be hiding.

Prop Storage

Prop Storage is the "closet" of the prop master — an enormous walk-in closet. With just a spoonful of sugar, prop storage would put Mary Poppins' carpetbag to shame. It is the place where you are bound to find anything and everything: props old and new, big and small, decorative and practical. The treasury of the prop department, prop storage shelters every tangible prop belonging to the theater company.

Typical Storage Spaces

Prop masters tend to agree when it comes to describing ideal prop storage: a climate-controlled, dust and pest free warehouse with rows upon rows of well-lit prop filing systems. A warehouse full of metal shelving, eight feet tall with rolling library ladders to reach the many organized options of each type of prop imaginable. An open view of the priceless collection of well-maintained sofas, settees, tables, and armchairs on display with specially designed cantilever racks that disappear into the horizon. Of course, there would also be a crew of prop people to pull and re-catalog the props for you. Ah, to dream.

In reality, prop storage places vary greatly. From converted old barns to lofts in dusty scene shops, prop storage consists of found spaces. Most prop departments have an enclosed area or two to store most of the non-furniture props in an effort to keep them contained and dust free. Set dressing, small set props, practicals, and hand props are organized on shelves and grouped with like items. Larger storage spaces such as outdoor storage units, barns, and garages are reserved for large set props and most pieces of furniture.

Unfortunately, it is not always the atypical wear and tear of stage blocking that is the main culprit for ruining props. The environment within the storage space can really do a number on them too. Humidity and heat warps wood, causes finishes to dull, and leaves fabrics with a constantly damp feeling. In places that never dry out, mold and mildew will overtake props in no time, rendering them unusable. Rodents, birds, moths, and other creatures can find homes in any kind of storage space regardless of location. I have reupholstered many sofas harboring mice nests in the cushions. Cleaning bird feces off of table tops and chair backs is a chore that can only be described as disgusting. Take my word for it —

if the theater can hire a pest control company to monitor prop storage spaces with regular visits, it is well worth the money.

What Props Should Be Stored

A great prop stock is full of props that could be used again in future productions or may bring in rental income. Depress the urge to fully unleash the "pack rat" inside of you. It is not practical to save every prop ever built or acquired. Not only would you run out of storage space, but you would end up with shelves of space-eating junk. As a rule of thumb, most props made specifically for one show that would almost never be rented or sold at a yard sale need to be pitched before they cross the storage threshold.

Do keep props that are hard to find. Usually rare antiques are good to hang on to. Antique or vintage pieces that are highly sought after are keepers — mainly because they would be impossible to find again for a few years. Do not keep a wide selection of modern furniture in stock, especially if your furniture storage is limited and your theater only produces modern plays once per season. Definitely keep props that are well-built, classic in style and function, and could potentially play in many historical settings. For a reminder of which kinds of props contribute to a great prop stock, check out Chapter 1.

Storage Organization and Inventory

It seems that no matter how ideal prop storage spaces are, in a flash they can change from wonderful and inviting to repulsive, disorganized, messy, and in need of constant attention. How your stock is organized depends on the size of your storage space, what props you have, and your personal tastes. As mentioned earlier, every prop department will be organized differently, but the same tip for organizing the workspace applies for the arrangement of small-props storage. Keep similar items and props that may fall into the same category together, or at least within close proximity of each other. Metal storage shelves, clear storage bins, drawer units, and shelf dividers are necessary if you want any kind of order. If you are stumped at how to even start organizing, begin by separating your props into the following categories:

Antique tools
Artificial flowers/foliage
Baskets
Dish sets
Electronics
Farming equipment
Gardening supplies
Kitchenware
Lighting
Miscellaneous
Office supplies
Paper props
Restaurant/bar equipment
Serving paraphernalia
Sporting goods
Toiletries
Vases
Weapons

Appliances
Bags
Books and magazines
Drinkware
Fake food
Frames
Glassware
Knickknacks
Medical/scientific
Musical instruments
Personal accessories
Religious
Rugs
Smoking accessories
Soft goods
Toys/games
Wall décor

Once your props are separated into sections, the order in which the props are placed on the shelves is the next challenge. Group props in the way that makes the best sense to you and to anyone else who may have to access prop storage. For example, luggage and bags could be shelved next to each other. Decorative items like wall décor, frames, knickknacks, religious items, and vases could each have a shelf within the same shelving unit. Another example would be to keep dish sets, drinkware, and kitchenware within proximity. All soft goods — towels, napkins, bed linen, tablecloths, curtains, etc. — would be happy to share a corner cabinet in storage. It is your space, and you should organize it however it makes sense to you.

Ideally, furniture stock would be stored in the same manner as smaller props, with the attempt to keep similar things together or at least in the same area. Organizing furniture storage can prove to be a little more challenging since furniture takes up a lot more space than small props. Sometimes stacking furniture is like a game of Tetris — a delicate puzzle of heavy and odd-shaped objects. Maximize your storage space by building platforms sturdy enough to support the weight of several pieces of furniture and tall enough

Chapter 6
Collections and Files

"What are these props supposed to look like?" Research collections are your very own private library and your keys to making every prop perfect and keeping embarrassment at bay. Gathering your collection won't happen overnight. However, resource and how-to books will start to fill up your bookshelves, your binders will bulge with every piece of information you come across, and your filing cabinets will brim over with handy paperwork.

Your Bookshelves

Even though the Internet can be a lifesaver in more ways than one, books remain incredibly valuable resources. Books take the guesswork out of many projects. The prop master dabbles in nearly every how-to project imaginable. Every propping project requires a little bit of research and a little bit of know-how. Specific books will guide you through each and every step of your task and answer your valuable questions. There is no better way to keep learning new ways of doing things than to keep cracking open the books.

Resource and how-to books can become your best friends. A book on molding and casting will patiently teach you how to cast the face of an actor, and won't get mad if you screw up. Not only can you look up information quickly, but books also travel nicely. You can take your historical furniture book with you to a production meeting to clear up an armchair discussion.

Books are hard workers, great teachers, and are always ready for action. Like cookbooks, how-to books don't complain if they get dirty. They live to get spilled on, written in, and marred up. Of course, library books seem to have a stuffy outlook on life and have consequences for dirtiness. Nonetheless, books are reliable. They will forever have the same information in them that they had two years ago when you last referenced them. Plus, books don't "bump you off" if the connection is lousy. Books provide a clear path to a forest of knowledge.

A Good Library Costs Money

Yes, books usually do cost money. For most of us, this puts limits on how fast and how often we can purchase books. A prop master's library is usually built one book at a time, and most books are acquired out of need. It is hard to foresee what types of books you may need down the road, or what subjects you will most likely need to reference time and again, especially if you are just beginning your career in props. Unfortunately, not every prop master has a resource materials line built into his budget. However, if the opportunity to rush out and buy numerous books presents itself, suggested books that can jump-start your library are mentioned in this chapter.

How to build your library:

- Purchase the books with your own money. Easy to say, but not always practical to do. If you buy books with your own money, ask to be reimbursed for the purchase if you don't intend to keep the book for yourself. If reimbursement is not an option, make sure you clearly indicate to whom the book belongs and remember to take it with you if you decide to move on to another workplace.

- Find money in the budget. Talk to your supervisor about your needs for resource materials. Your supervisor will either help create a budget for future expenses or help determine where the money could come from.

- Seek out yard sales and resale shops for great deals.

- Start a book donation drive. Involve the theater community by asking patrons and businesses to donate new or used resource and how-to books. Provide a list of needed books and an opportunity for them to get the books to you, either personally or via a convenient drop-off location.

- Work with your development department. Would this department be able to find and apply for a grant or monetary donation solely intended for your prop library? It never hurts to ask.

How-To Books

Books on how to make things or do certain tasks are available in large numbers. The variety of subjects covered is amazing. You can teach yourself how to glue popsicle sticks together, replicate antique furniture, or design and create outlandish special effects. Even if you don't have the time to read, most how-to books are designed to help you understand certain processes in the most efficient way.

Suggestions for Your How-To Book Collection

Book making	Crafts and hobbies
Doll making	Furniture building
Metal working	Prop making
Soft goods construction	Sewing and quilting
Scenic art	Scenic design
Special effects	Upholstery
Woodworking	

Reference Books

You can find a book that covers just about anything you would like to research. Libraries are full of research books, but having a collection of your own is better. Retail bookstores and online booksellers offer an enormous variety of research books. Most resources are found in the nonfiction areas that include sections such as art, antiques and collectibles, food and wine, history, and home and garden.

Reference books give you the most accurate pictorial view of history. Since being a historian is one of the hats a prop master wears, it only makes sense that you surround yourself with the appropriate resources. The pictures in these books also assist you in making your props look as "vintage" as possible. (Always be mindful of copyright laws.)

Suggestions for Your Reference Book Collection

Art and architecture	Backstage handbook
Cigarettes	Coins and currency
Dover publications	Furniture
Gardening	Luggage labels
Musical instruments	Old bottles
Sears 1897 catalog	Stamps

Surfaces   Theater books
Vintage item books   Weapons
Wine, beer, and liquor

Catalogs

Even though catalogs aren't books, they are exceptional resources. Retail, wholesale, and trade catalogs should have a special place in your office. Just like books, catalogs offer a quick search to finding what you need to buy. Over time, you will find that you use certain catalogs more than others. Most companies will keep you in their database if you continue to order from them. As new catalogs come in, either throw away the old ones or file them with your resource books for photo references. The worst thing when ordering supplies or props is to find out that you're using an old catalog and the company no longer carries what you need.

Suggested Types of Retail and Supply Catalogs

Antique replicas   Art and craft supply
Artificial floral   Hardware
Industrial   Lighting
Party supply and novelties
Weapons retail and rental
Wholesale furniture (finished, unfinished, kits)
Furniture retailers
Wholesale visual merchandise

There are many easy ways to start collecting catalogs. Your prop shop may already have a great collection to look through. Contact other prop masters to see what catalogs and companies they use. You can also search the Internet for catalogs. In a search engine, type in the genre of catalog you wish to find. For example: "Artificial Flowers" or "Silk Flowers." Most of the larger companies will be listed, and once you visit their website you can sign up to receive their catalog. However, there are a few companies that ask that you purchase something from their website before they will send you their valuable catalog.

Research Collections

Research collections are your excuse for why you hang on to the coffee-stained and torn piece of tablet paper that offers the secret recipe for producing the most brilliant pyro effect ever; the accidental picture of alley garbage you took on your vacation, but referenced when you propped *Cats*; the handout from the paint store with the faux finishing instructions you followed to give your furniture the perfect look for *The Price*. The simple explanation of why you keep this information is that you needed this stuff at one point, and you'll most likely need this stuff again.

Research collections are paper files of things you come across in your research travels and know will be of some use in the future. These could be magazine articles, ads, pictures, newspaper articles, photographs, craft instructions, pamphlets, brochures, photocopies, and all of the information you've saved from previous shows.

A great way to keep these loose papers and pamphlets together is with three-ring binders, subject dividers, and glossy transparent protective sheets. Or, stick with your bent manila folders that rarely hold onto all of your papers. The choice is yours.

Your Filing Cabinet

Every prop master has her own organizational preferences and uses for a filing cabinet. Some use the cabinet for extra prop storage, others use it to store work clothes and snacks. Some store their catalogs, research files, contacts and databases, and company paperwork in the drawers. Again, the choice is yours.

Contacts

E-mail addresses, phone numbers, mailing addresses, primary contacts, and directions will begin to spill out of your filing cabinet over time. Accumulate lists of all the people, stores, and interesting places you encounter or come across during your propping adventures. Of course, you'll want to keep your lists organized and accessible so you can update your lists and check them regularly.

A Stockpile of Contacts

Antique/resale shops	Appliance stores
Area prop masters	Craft stores
Designers	Directors
Fabric stores	Freelance artisans
Hardware stores	Local theaters
Masters of the trade	Regional theaters
Rental houses	Repair shops
Professional theater companies	
Prop master support groups	

Company Papers

There isn't a company in the world that doesn't have paperwork, records, reports, forms, letters, and form letters. These companies have a knack for making their employees be passionate about paperwork, too. Since there is no possible way to avoid the paperwork — the blank forms, the filled-out forms, and all the copies of the filled-out forms — it makes sense to organize it all and file it away.

The prop master has managerial responsibilities to the prop department that revolve around the masses of company paperwork. Tracking and reporting expenditures to the finance department and the production manager requires the use of many forms. Most theaters have their own versions and formats of the forms they use, but they are all roughly the same. Some of the forms in this section may be helpful to you if your theater does not have its own standard forms or methods of tracking and sharing information.

Standard Prop Shop Paperwork:

Purchase Orders

A purchase order, or P.O., is a two- or three-page carbonless document that a buyer uses as a legal promise to pay a seller for certain goods. Purchase orders are often used when you have an account with a vendor and plan to have the vendor bill you later. Once you turn in copies of the purchase order to the finance department, they can match up the purchase order numbers and pay the bill. Purchase orders can also be used for any credit card charges made to the theater's accounts. All receipts are stapled to the business copy of the purchase order.

83

Purchase orders are usually half the size of regular copy paper and have the company logo or address printed on them. The information you may need to fill out is your name, theater department, and date of purchase order. List the items you have purchased, the quantity, the price per item, and the account code indicating from which budget line the money will be taken. Purchase orders are usually double-signed by the department head and his direct supervisor as an accounting security practice. Keep a copy of the P.O. before turning it in to the finance department.

Petty Cash Reimbursement

Petty cash reimbursement forms keep track of receipt amounts and state which account will have the total applied, while indicating to the finance department the amount of money you need to have reimbursed. These types of forms can work for theater petty cash and credit card reimbursements or for reimbursing yourself if you used your personal funds to purchase props or supplies. As discussed in Chapter 4, petty cash is an amount of money in the form of cash that is assigned to you by the theater (if your theater gives you cash as a means for purchasing props). Figure 6.1 provides an example form.

PETTY CASH REIMBURSEMENT FORM

NAME: _____ DATE: _____

DATE	PLACE	AMOUNT	ACCT CODE

TOTAL AMOUNT SPENT: _____

ACCT CODE #:	AMOUNT SPENT: $
ACCT CODE #:	AMOUNT SPENT: $
ACCT CODE #:	AMOUNT SPENT: $

Figure 6.1

84

Budget Spreadsheets

Budget spreadsheets are the best way to keep track of all of your department's expenses. These forms track purchase orders and cash receipts and are similar to a check register, only they record more information concerning your purchases. Keeping a good record of your expenditures will help you stay within your budget and help solve any budgeting discrepancies that may arise between you, your boss, and the finance department. Each budget line should have its own spreadsheet per show. Typical prop shop budgets include lines for materials, travel, labor, and prop shop supplies. You may have more lines to control if you have a company vehicle to look after, etc. (More budget line information can be found in Chapter 4.) Figure 6.2 provides abbreviated examples of functional ways to set up budget spreadsheets for the materials, labor, and travel budgets.

BUDGET SPREADSHEET EXAMPLES

Name of Theater Company   Account Code #: 4500. 01
Title of Production   **MATERIALS BUDGET: $1000.00**

DATE	ITEM	CASH/PO	PLACE	COST	SPENT	REMAIN
5/02	Furniture Rental	PO 6744	The Prop Place Rentals	$500.00	$500.00	$500.00
5/04	Fabric, thread, upholstery foam	PO 6745	The Fabric Store	$75.00	$575.00	$425.00
5/04	Candles, matches,	PO 6747	The Candle Store	$9.00	$584.00	$416.00

LABOR BUDGET: $800.00

DATE	NAME	HOURS	RATE	AMOUNT	PO #	SPENT	REMAIN
5/10	Ima Propman	10	$15.00 p/h	$150.00	PO 6751	$150.00	$650.00

TRAVEL BUDGET: $200.00

DATE	NAME	PO #	AMOUNT	SPENT	REMAIN
5/04	Gas for company van	PO 6746	$90.00	$90.00	$110.00
5/12	Mileage reimbursement for Joe	PO 6753	$70.00	$160.00	$40.00

Figure 6.2

85

Vacation Request Forms

When you plan for your vacations you will need to provide the dates of your vacation to your supervisor. An easy way to do this is with a simple document with spaces for your name and position, dates you request off, and lines for you and your boss to sign and date. These forms are easy to make and will create a paper trail. How horrifying would it be to come back from a scheduled vacation and not have a job because your boss didn't know where you were?

New Hire Forms

The theater's finance department and your supervisor should have current federal and state regulated new hire forms on hand. You will only need these forms when you hire a freelance artist or if you are directly responsible for hiring the prop department staff. For tax and work authorization purposes, the newly hired employee will most likely be asked to fill out the Federal Withholding Certificate (W-4) along with any state forms and the Employment Eligibility Verification (I-9). These forms should be turned in to the finance department before any time sheets are turned in.

Tax Exempt Letters

A tax exemption is a release from paying certain state or federal taxes that most businesses or individuals would normally have to pay. Non-profit organizations are normally granted tax-exempt status by governments in an effort to reduce the tax burden on organizations whose activities benefit certain segments or interests of society. Organizations such as theaters and schools who can prove non-profit status can apply for tax exemption for states they do business with frequently. If approved, the organization will receive confirmation via letter from the issuing state. How does this help the prop master? Sales tax can really eat a chunk out of your budget lines. Showing a copy of this letter to vendors can reduce your total spending costs. Some wholesale suppliers will not sell their wares unless you can prove you are affiliated with an actual business. Providing the company's federal identification number or a copy of the tax exempt letter will help you get through the red tape.

Volunteer Indemnification Agreement

A volunteer indemnification agreement can be used when volunteers, or people who are not employed by the theater company, perform work or engage in any activity in the prop shop (or any other department of the theater). It is a security measure the theater takes to keep from being held responsible (or sued) should anything happen to harm the volunteer while on the company's premises, using the company's tools, breathing the air of the company's building, etc. Most indemnification agreements are short letters filled with one run-on sentence of complete legal jargon. The theater powers-that-be should make sure this type of letter is provided. Lawyers are paid big money to draft these agreements; writing your own is not the way to go. I took the liberty of making up a fake agreement for example purposes. If you imagine that the words in Figure 6.5 are more complex and confusing than they are, you will have a better sense of what a real agreement would be like. Do not use, copy, reference, or distribute this example.

Volunteer Indemnification Agreement

I, _____, (Name of Volunteer) am volunteering my time to the Theater within the _____ (Title of Theater Department) department on this day and between these hours_____ (Date and Time) and understand as a condition of the Theater's permission to allow any volunteer activity, I shall indemnify, and hold harmless the Theater and its employees, board of directors, and other volunteers in regards to any loss, damage, or injury that is because of, or is in any way related to, my acts while participating in the volunteer activity.

Date _____

Name of Volunteer _____

Signature of Volunteer _____

Address of Volunteer _____

_____

Figure 6.5

Rental Agreement

When other companies, theaters, schools, or individuals borrow or rent props or tools from your department, it is wise to have the person responsible for borrowing or renting fill out a rental agreement. The same applies when you borrow or rent items from other companies, theaters, schools, or individuals. The rental agreement serves many purposes and covers the details agreed upon between the organization and the renter.

The rental agreement primarily sets down the rules and terms of the rental. It will state whether you are borrowing (using something for free) or renting (paying a fee to the renter). It is a record of who you are, where to find you, what you're borrowing, how long you intend to borrow it, and your promise to return it in the same condition you borrowed it (unless otherwise discussed and agreed to by the theater) by the date specified, or you will pay the fines or fees as outlined in the agreement.

Both the theater and the renter/borrower should sign and date the agreement and keep a copy for themselves. If you are borrowing something from someone who does not have a specific agreement, create one. The rental agreement not only protects the person who is loaning, but can also keep the renter out of trouble. Figure 6.6 is a standard rental agreement in the propping industry.

COMPANY

LOGO/ADDRESS

LETTER OF AGREEMENT

(CIRCLE ONE)

RENTAL AGREEMENT/ BORROWING AGREEMENT

NAME OF RENTER

POSITION TITLE

NAME OF ORGANIZATION

PHONE NUMBER

ADDRESS

START DATE OF RENTAL

RETURN DATE OF RENTAL

DEPOSIT AMOUNT

TOTAL RENTAL COSTS

The Renter agrees to the following:

1. All Theater property used by Renter will be returned in the same condition as noted at start date of rental.
2. Any alterations to the condition of Theater property must have written Theater permission.
3. All Theater property used by Renter will be returned by date specified above, unless other arrangements are agreed to.
4. Theater property not returned by date specified above is subject to 3% of the value of each item used multiplied by each day Theater Property is past due.
5. Renter will pay to Theater full cost value of any Theater Property that is broken, damaged, or considered lost by Renter and will forfeit the deposit amount. Theater has sole discretion in determining Theater Property damage that does not fall in line with what is generally considered normal wear and tear.
6. All rental costs will be paid in full by Renter to Theater within one week of rental start date as specified above.

PROPERTY	DESCRIPTION	CONDITION	VALUE $

Agreed to and Signed by:

Signature of Theater

Signature of Renter

Date

Date

Figure 6.6

Chapter 7
The First Steps of the Build Process

"How do I know what props to find?"
Read the script. Take notes on props
mentioned in the script and study the
information the designers and director have
provided. Create a prop list and put all of
your information in a binder so that none
of these precious materials will be lost.
Determine if you have enough time and
talent to get the show propped and a
budget big enough to fit the bill.

Collecting Prop Data

There are two parts to the entire propping process: The
preliminary preparation process and the prop build — the physical
propping work. The prep work is just as vital to the show as
acquiring the props is. Both parts of the process are interrelated,
meaning that the first part benefits the second part and the second
part benefits the first. It is the first part, the preliminary work, that
will pull you through the entire propping process without feeling
like you want to run from your office screaming, "*I quit!*"

Preliminary work gives you a chance to acquaint yourself with
the project and plan what you'll be working on for the next six
weeks or so. Reading the script, meeting the set designer and
director, and discussing the concept and show designs are important
for collecting prop data. The other half of the preliminary process
allows you to view the bigger picture and study the possibilities in
terms of budget, time, and labor. Then you can determine if these
resources will support the show's prop needs.

Read the Script

First things first — read the script twice. Why twice? The first
time you read the script is for the sheer enjoyment of it. Like
reading a novella, you'll get a great sense of what the play is about,
what the characters are like, where they live, and why they live the
way they do. You will grasp the overall feeling — the mood of the

play and the moral of the story (if there is one).

Grab your legal pad and a pen because the second read is for seriously dealing with the details in the play. As you make your way through the script, stop at every prop reference. Write down every prop mentioned on your legal pad. Note the page number where the prop is mentioned, which character handles the prop, and any particular details the script gives about the prop or how it is used.

Finding Props in the Script

Props can be found throughout the script. Props are mentioned in the setting and character descriptions, the stage directions, and in the dialogue. Not all plays are created equal. Some playwrights are so detailed with their prop descriptions that there is no margin for creative deviation. On the other side of the equation, Shakespeare's plays barely have any stage directions, and the props discussed in the dialogue are sometimes rather vague.

In the following examples, props will be underlined every time they are mentioned.

The **setting description**, found on the first page of the script, provides insight into the historical time period, location, and mood of the play. Depending on how detailed this description is, there may be mention of set props and dressing and maybe a hand or costume prop as well.

Script Example:

At the beginning of the play, the light of early morning bounces off the rusty screen door — the only entrance to the dilapidated two-story farmhouse. The year is 1939 and <u>farm implements, tools, scrap metal</u>, and <u>rubbish</u> are strewn about the tiny front yard. Mable appears in the doorway, looking exhausted, grasping her <u>cup of coffee</u> with her two hands.

The **character descriptions**, also found near the beginning of the script, provide socio-economic status, age, occupations, a glimpse into the character's psyche, and, if you're lucky, the revealing of a costume prop.

Script Example:
Mable is 41 yrs. old and tired down to her bones. Widowed at 24, she was forced to raise three boys on a dime. Her home, her possessions, even her land look worn out. Only her morning <u>cup of coffee</u> and the <u>Bible</u> in her apron pocket bring her comfort.

Stage directions are blocking notes, technical cues, and instructions found throughout the dialogue of the script, which are written in italics and/or in parentheses. Oftentimes props can be found in the stage directions along with clues about the condition of the prop.

Script Example:
MABLE: You hungry? *(Mable turns to Joe, holding her <u>half-eaten sandwich</u>.)*

The **dialogue**, or words the characters speak, makes up the body of the script. It is usually where most props are mentioned, including certain details.

Script example:
MABLE: Eat your <u>sandwich</u>, Joe. And here. Have this <u>Hershey kiss from my pocket</u>. Sorry. <u>It melted into a chocolate foil pancake</u>.

Reading the script is important. The prop master's responsibility is to be fully engaged in the projects of the production. Reading the script will allow for more intelligent conversations with the director and designer about the show. If you don't understand the plot of the play after reading it, ask someone to give you a synopsis or conduct your own research. After all, the play and the performance are the reasons why there is a need for props.

The Script's Prop List
As a general rule of thumb, prop masters rarely make prop notes based on the prop list found in the back of the published script. (We might sneak a peak at it, but that's it.)

The prop list in the script was from the original production of the play. Your theater's production of the same play will have a different design and concept to drive the prop choices than the original did. You may not even need half of the props this list mentions, and it is best to just ignore it.

Propping a play with no script

There are productions that don't have scripts to study — just a troupe of performers and a creative idea to start. The idea may evolve into a written script or may remain improvised throughout the performances. If you are the prop master for this process, most likely you are aware of the constant creative challenges developing a show like this will entail: You may not be able to create a preliminary prop list. Your prop list will grow larger the farther into the rehearsal process you get. You must stay in communication with the director, stage manager, and set designer for prop changes and additions and keep your prop list updated. Creative production processes like this pose occasional propping challenges and a faster-paced propping process than usual. A process like this will be very rewarding if you remain flexible and are working with a director and other artists who are aware of the reality of time and budget when they make their prop requests.

Noting Prop Specifics

Period/Style

The period of the play is usually stated. As you are writing down props and taking notes on their specifics, keep the historical period of the play in mind. The time period will help narrow down the style of furniture and other props that could be used in the show. Your designer will be able to pinpoint exactly what style he's thinking of for the various props, but getting your own sense of the period and style will aid you in your conversations with the designer.

There are occasions when the director decides to "shake things up" and set the play in a completely different time period than the one for which it was originally set or written. This happens with Shakespeare's plays more often than not. If you are at all unsure of the time period of your production, move this question to the top of list of things to discuss with your director.

Function/Action

Props that are actually mentioned in the script usually have a specific function pertaining to the action of the play. These props are meant to do more than just "sit there." Reading the script will allow you to discern the importance of a prop's function and whether the prop will require special attention. Note on your legal pad whatever information you can glean about a prop and the circumstances that may affect the prop.

A prop with a very minor role (an end table, for example) that will only be expected to function as it would in everyday life may not be that noteworthy. However, a typical armchair used for sitting during most of the show and then danced on by the portly chef during the last scene should be given much consideration. This chair would need to be reinforced and monitored throughout the show for structural integrity. Newspaper props stating specific headlines might have to be realistic, especially if these props are closely viewable by the audience.

Consumable props have special functions; some are torn, some are thrown, and some are consumed. The fact of the matter is that these props will be severely affected by the action of the play. These props will need replacements, and the importance of this should be noted.

Special effects are props whose functions in the play need to be recorded. If it shoots, catches fire, creates smoke, changes shape, or performs a trick, you can count on it needing extra attention and extra planning. Notes about these props should be jotted down on your legal pad and underlined.

All of these notes you've taken on prop function and action will assist you with planning a little later on in the process. Based on your notes and the information you get from the director and set designer, you will be better equipped to create your plan of attack for acquiring or building these props.

Study the Designs

Six weeks to two months before opening night, the set designer sends his final designs (via digital or hard copy) to the theater in time for the build to begin. Get your hands on a copy of the entire design and set aside time to study the plans and drawings so you can make detailed notes. All sorts of prop data will be uncovered and extracted from the designs. You may find answers to some of the initial questions you had after reading the script in these designs. Or you may wind up with more items to discuss.

Set designs will offer the following prop information:
- Size, style, period, position, and amount of set props and dressing.
- Mood and feeling of play's environment.
- Class, financial status, and personality of the characters.
- Historical period and location of the play.

Components of a Set Design

You'll find that all designers are different, not only in personality and how they prefer things to be done, but more importantly in what information about the set they provide to the theater. In addition to scenic building plans and drawings, some designers may provide color renderings and three-dimensional models depicting how the finished set will look. Even more ambitious designers will also see to it that the prop shop is given lists and research for set dressing and, in very rare cases, the designer will provide his own compiled prop list.

Ground Plan

The ground plan is a scale drawing, used by nearly all production departments as a reference for how the set will be placed on the stage. It is drawn as a bird's eye view, or top view, of the set. This is exceptionally handy for the prop master to determine what set props and large set dressing props are expected to be on the set and the approximate footprint of each prop. Although fictional, Figure 7.1 provides a sample ground plan set in a basic proscenium theater.

Set Elevations

Set elevations are detailed scale drawings that contain pertinent size and construction information used for building the set. Elevations show off the front and side views of each section of the set as if the piece had been flattened into two dimensions. Oftentimes, if there is a specially designed prop for the show, the designer will go ahead and include the elevations for it in his design package. Figure 7.2 is a good example of an elevation for a prop bench.

97

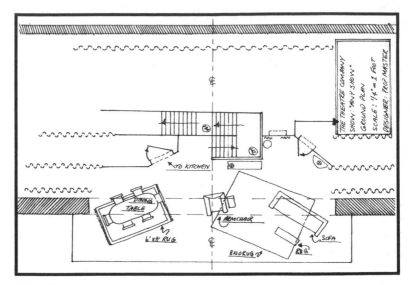

Figure 7.1

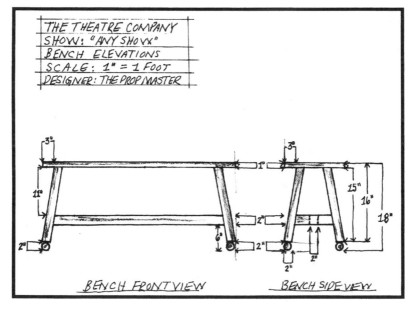

THE THEATRE COMPANY
SHOW: "ANY SHOVX"
BENCH ELEVATIONS
SCALE: 1" = 1 FOOT
DESIGNER: THE PROP MASTER

BENCH FRONT VIEW   BENCH SIDE VIEW

Figure 7.1

Paint Elevations

Paint elevations are front view, scale drawings depicting the exact colors and painting techniques desired for each set piece. Paint elevations are given to the scenic artist. The prop master should view these elevations as another way to stay on top of the final picture for the set. The prop staff may reference the color palette time and again through the propping process.

Model

The set model is an exact three-dimensional, miniature, or scale replica of the ground plan and elevations created to provide the production and artistic staff with an idea of how the set will look and/or function on-stage. The model is usually housed within a model box, which is a scale replica of the actual stage where the set will be loaded. Model boxes are simply made, lack detail, and painted black in order to show off the model inside.

Models are usually constructed with full detail, texture choices, and the color palette the designer would like to see reflected on the real set pieces. Oftentimes detailed models are used as a replacement for paint elevations, and vice versa.

A white model is a simple, three-dimensional scale replica of the set that lacks detail, color, and texture. White models are sometimes made to double check how set pieces will fit together on-stage and to save time and money on modeling materials.

Models are a great reference for the prop department. Most size, shape, style, or color questions can be answered by studying the model.

Rendering

A set rendering is a sketch or detailed, colored, two-dimensional drawing of the set from the audience's perspective. It is often used in conjunction with a white model. In an effort to save time, designers sometimes choose to provide a colored rendering instead of a model. Although renderings are usually visually interesting, they are not the most ideal reference tool for the prop shop. Prop and scenery sizes may get distorted in the designer's attempt to convey the overall mood or spirit of the show.

Set Research Pictures

Research pictures gleaned from books or the Internet may be offered by the designer. These are used mostly by the set and paint shops for detail and texture reference. Just another bit of information for the prop master to check out.

Prop Research

The designer may provide pictorial information portraying the period and style of set props and set dressing that she hopes the prop master will be able to acquire for the show. Hand prop research may also be included. This information makes your job a lot easier, saving you the time of researching these props yourself.

Create the Prop List

Once you have read the script, studied the ground plans, and have a healthy amount of notes on your legal pad, it is time to transfer all that data and information to the prop list. The prop list is a record and a reference of all the props needed for the entire production. This includes all hand, set, and set dressing props as well as costume, consumable, practical, and special effect props.

This list should be organized chronologically in keeping with the course of action in the play. It will continually evolve to reflect prop changes requested throughout the rehearsal process. The prop list is not the same as a grocery list or a "to do" list. Anyone who picks up a prop list should be able to determine in what act and page the prop appears, which character uses the prop, and any detailed information regarding the prop. This list is the most important document the prop master will produce.

Set designers and directors might send you their versions of the prop list. Knowing what props the director and designer ultimately want for the production is key. However, these lists are usually incomplete. Directors seem to have an affinity for hand prop specifics, which their list will reflect, and designers can be just the opposite, with their lists full of set prop and dressing details. The best plan of attack is to combine their lists and notes and add them to your preliminary prop list.

I consider the first version of the prop list the "preliminary prop list." In my opinion, the "final" prop list is the one that kicks off the main event of the opening night performance. Any list before that is in a constant state of change and may only be used as a reference and record for the work up to the opening. Please assume that when I mention the prop list from here on out, I am referring to the preliminary version unless I state otherwise.

A sample prop list is shown in Figure 7.3. Using a computer spreadsheet program to create a prop list template will make transferring your notes to the prop list much easier, trust me. Title your list with theater's name, show title, and date. This is so others may quickly find your list if necessary. Begin the process of converting your handwritten notes into the official prop list. Separate props that are set and dressing props and arrange them at the beginning of the list. If set props or set dressing props are mentioned somewhere in the script, note the page number. After that, copy over your hand prop notes in the order in which they appear in the script starting with Act 1.

Every prop master likes to do things his own way, and there is no official way of creating a prop list. But why deviate from what works? Please feel free to use the example in Figure 7.3 as a guide or template.

Name of Theater Company
Title of Production
Preliminary Props List
Date of List Creation

PAGE	PROP	CHARACTER	NOTES
	SET PROPS		
	Upholstered loveseat		SR, wooden frame, light brown upholstery
	End table		SL of loveseat
	Sofa table		Behind loveseat, narrow and slightly lower than back of sofa
	Armchair		SL recovered in sepia toned fabric
	Bookcase		SL of armchair. Dk. Wood
	Dining table		Dk. Wood, oval. Lightweight for actors to carry. Placed SL
	Dining chairs		Dk. Wood. Brought onstage by actors to SL
	SET DRESSING		
	Ashtray		On end table
	Picture frames		On end table and sofa table
	Files and papers		Messy, on dining table
	Coffee cup		Preset on sofa table
	Hanging picture frames		Sepia toned, see elevation and model for details
	Bookcase dressing		Books, knickknacks, pictures
	Table lamp		Practical, middle sofa table
	Telephone		Rings. Set on end table; 1940 s period. Black.
	ACT I sc. 1		
	HAND PROPS		
10	Newspaper	Sarah	1940 s. Jacksonville, FL. No other specifics
14	Bible	Robert	
14	Car keys	Robert	
16	Birthday present	Sarah	Small tie box, brown paper wrapping w/ string
17	Needlepoint	Sarah	with hoop, already started
17	Needlepoint bag	Sarah	
19	Crossword puzzle	Robert	Folded newspaper page w/crossword; consumable
20	Money	Robert	various amounts, several bills

Figure 7.3

Contact Designers and Directors

Throughout the entire production process, communication with the set designer and director is mandatory. Your partnership in helping to realize the design is essential. (Avoiding the designer and director is an immature move that can land you in some hot water.) The creative design team places a lot of trust in the prop master and other department heads. They are going to share information down to the tiniest detail because they want you to be an enlightened and reliable team member who is on the same creative page and working toward the same artistic goal. Make yourself available for conversations; better yet, make the first move.

Share your preliminary prop list with both the director and designer. Let them know that the list you have sent to them has been compiled from reading the script, studying the designs, and adding in the prop information both of them may have supplied to you. Ask them to look the prop list over and add, change, or remove props as they see fit. Tell them that you would love to schedule a phone call or, if possible, an in-person meeting to review the list and discuss the show.

Designers and directors will normally respond to your initiated "hello" quite promptly. Discussions with these two artists are not only informative, but can also be positively entertaining as you receive the inside scoop behind the concept and design inspirations and decisions. Take copious notes. This is the time to have them explain why your production of *Hamlet* is set in 1950s small-town America. These chats can clear up all sorts of confusion you had about the show, the production, and the props. Don't be shy — ask the questions for which you need answers; get the information you need. These chats will prompt designers to provide you with research or pertinent drawings if they haven't already. Right after you have these initial conversations, transfer this new prop information into the preliminary prop list.

The Prop Bible

The "prop bible" is prop-speak for the revered reference binder you create to hold every piece of prop information which crosses your desk. The importance of being an organized prop master cannot be stressed enough, and this reference binder is another way to show off your organizational talents. Nothing is more helpful than knowing where much-sought-after prop data has wound up. If you have stored copies of your files, research, lists, and notes in one complete binder, you will never experience the frustration of not being able to find the designer's phone number or the designs for building the Art Deco china cabinet. Like everything else in theater, the information in the prop bible will change and be added to as prop production work progresses.

The prop bible is a three-ring binder with plastic pockets and a spine width of at least one-and-a-half inches. It is not the binder that is important; it is what is inside that counts. Organized in a way that works best for each prop master, assembly of the prop bible should commence as soon as work begins on the show, if not earlier. Plastic sheet protectors are perfect for keeping your paper research and lists safe from tears or spills and for combining several pages into a see-through pocket.

A typical prop bible holds the following bits of useful information:

- Copy of the script.
- Current copy of the production calendar.
- Contact sheet (production and guest artist contact information).
- Up-to-date copy of the prop list.
- Notes from reading the script.
- Notes or lists from the designer and director.
- Minimized copies of set ground plan, renderings, and prop elevations.
- Prop research from the designer.
- Prop research conducted by the prop master.
- Paint and fabric color swatches.
- Copies of e-mails to and from the designer and director.
- Copies of the rehearsal report.
- Paperwork important to prop production.

Copies of financial records and receipts should be kept in the prop bible only if you choose. I prefer to keep these two types of data separate. If I misplaced the prop bible, I wouldn't risk losing the financial records also. The prop bible is often viewed by other production team members; it travels to production meetings and might go on prop hunting tours with you. Financial records don't like adventures and are safest when kept in the office.

Studying the Possibilities

After the preliminary prop list has been created and you have a good perception of script, design, and concept requirements, carve out a chunk of time to dissect the prop list. You will need to take into account what each prop will require of your time, money, and materials. Do the initial prop requests seem reasonable? Do you have enough manpower and talent to get the jobs done? Can you afford to do this show?

Foresight: What Will Affect Your Work?

Before any propping work commences, take an initial analysis of how the resources available to you might influence the way in which you prop the show. Two major factors affect your prop work — budget and time — and it is good practice to make fairly accurate estimations of availability or constraints. Determining whether the prop list and your resources are realistic is fundamental to your efforts.

Budget

Show and department budgets are determined by a crew of theater managers, but it is usually your supervisor who shares your show budget amounts with you. As discussed in Chapter 4, the budget reflects either the actual or estimated money amounts allocated for use in the prop department.

Besides getting the show propped on time, another goal the prop master shoots for is keeping the costs of the show within the budget provided. Money has a huge effect on how the show is propped. It sets limits on spending and determines your propping plan of attack: what you can buy and what stores you can buy it from; what you can build, what materials you can use, and whether you can afford to hire an artisan to help; and what you will have to borrow, find, beg, or steal.

As a good rule of thumb, immediately shave 25% off your budget. Mentally set this amount aside to be used as a buffer or for last-minute prop expenses. If your prop materials budget is $1000, tell yourself you only have $750 to work with. Chances are you will wind up using your buffer before all is said and done, but will still close out the show under budget. If you do come in under budget, you can award yourself bonus points for good planning and luck.

Can You Afford the Show?

Before you spend a dime, create a cost-breakdown chart. With your prop list beside you, estimate any labor and material expenditures that each prop will require. Figure 7.4 is a cost breakdown chart, and you are welcome to replicate and expand this condensed format. Utilizing this chart will get easier as you become better acquainted with the typical costs of items and supplies.

Prop Cost Breakdown

PROP	B,B,B,P	MATERIALS	ESTIMATED	ACTUAL
Library Table	Build	1 sheet Plywood	$30.00	
		20' 1 x 6	$20.00	
		4 legs	$200.00	
Rug	Borrow		$50.00	
Suitcase	Pull		$0.00	
Account Page	Build	Paper, ink	$0.00	
Garden Book	Buy		$7.00	
		TOTAL ESTIMATED COSTS:	$307.00	
		TOTAL ACTUAL COSTS:		

Figure 7.4

Online research will also answer cost questions. It is better to estimate on the high end, of course. When you start to spend money, keep track of the actual costs on the breakdown sheet. Having these numbers side by side provides an excellent cost reference that can be used for future shows.

After you have combed through your entire prop list, add up the estimated costs. If the approximate cost of items and supplies is over budget, revisit your estimations. Can any props be borrowed instead of bought? Is it cheaper to buy instead of build, or vice versa? If your estimations are still coming in over budget, have your supervisor look at the props list vs. the cost breakdown estimations. He may find errors or offer other propping solutions. Nevertheless, he is now aware of your potential budget problems.

In dire circumstances, your supervisor may have the means to increase your prop budget. Never assume that this is a possibility. Don't wait until the dress rehearsal to announce that you don't have enough money to finish propping the show. This will not go over well. Like a fortune-teller, peer into your crystal ball and foresee (at least a couple of weeks in advance) if you will need to ask your boss for more money.

Time and Ability

Another resource that could obstruct the propping process is time. Do you have enough time to prop this show? Look at your production calendar. How many work days or weeks do you have before you need to start meeting prop deadlines? Will you have to put in overtime or work on the weekends?

To the best of your ability, create an initial project timetable. Estimating the amount of time you need for projects is a little more difficult than estimating expenditures because there are more variables. Variables which throw off or affect the time you have for projects could be any combination of things — having to run errands, traffic congestion, tool malfunction, crafts not coming together as quickly as expected, lack of assistance, and so on. If you don't take time into consideration, you will run out of it. Performance dates never change as a result of props being incomplete.

If you can afford the show and have enough time to prop the show, do you have enough people with the right skills to help out? Additional help greatly increases the time you have to get projects done, especially if the artisans possess the level of talent and know-how to positively assist you and accurately complete the assigned projects.

Time-saving tips: Set aside certain days or times of day for shopping trips. Organize your shopping lists ahead of time, know what stores you want to hit, and plan out your route. When building or crafting props, gather all your materials and tools for each project into accessible locations — this prevents you from wasting time searching for what you need. Don't procrastinate.

What is the Consensus?

Is Propping This Show Possible?

If your supervisor has looked at the cost breakdown and time estimates, and both of you determine that your budget is not large enough to prop the show and cannot be increased, the designer and director should be brought into the conversation. Designers and directors, for the most part, are willing to adjust the design and prop lists to something more manageable with your resources, and they may help you consider propping options you may not have thought about.

A warning: Never use budget or time constraints as a means to "get out of" having to work on or provide a prop. If you don't want to provide a prop just because you're exhausted, find your replacement and kindly take your leave. If budget and time constraints are legitimate reasons for not being able to do work, explain this to the director or designer but be prepared to provide or consider alternative propping solutions.

Raising Your Red Flag

I was told by a director once that I didn't "raise my red flag" early enough in the propping process for a prop concern to be resolved "in time." It is true that this particular prop was not completely finished until the afternoon of the first preview performance, and the actors never had the time to rehearse with it. In theater,  this is a very bad situation. In my defense, this was an exceptionally prop-heavy show, with many special effects, I was a department of one, blah, blah, blah ...

However, his constructive criticism has stuck with me, and I appreciate him saying what he did. During that show, as I was drowning myself in props, I regretted not having the foresight to imagine how difficult propping this show would become. I did not plan ahead. I did not share my concern about the complexities of this show and its particular props with my boss and director in enough time for them to help me figure out a resolution. Because I didn't share my concerns early on — did not "raise my red flag" — the director and set designer assumed all was well. Instead, their visions for the design and concept of the show took a hit.

Take this tip from my experience: If you have legitimate concerns, *especially* early on, don't hesitate to speak up. If you fear that you won't have (a) enough material or labor money, (b) time or resources, and/or (c) enough know-how or experience to get a project completed in time, share this information! Use good judgment — you'll want to avoid trying to make a big deal out of nothing or "crying wolf," but you don't want to regret keeping mum either. Your supervisor, director, and designer will appreciate your honest concern, and you will appreciate their expertise and resolutions.

Share Your Information

Once the prop list is approved, and/or revised by the director and designer and the props look like they will fit into the available resources, you're nearly ready to start "propping"! Just a couple more steps before you can begin.

Provide copies of your prop list to pertinent production department heads and guest artists. Sharing your prop list is another way of trying to keep the production team in sync. If the lighting designer or electrics department need to know how many practical props are designed into the show, they can reference the prop list. The choreographer can look at the list to determine what props might be available to incorporate into the dances. Stage management uses the prop list in many ways — to track when props are used in the show and where they will "live" backstage or in the rehearsal hall and to keep an eye out for which props still need to be supplied to rehearsal. The revised and updated prop list should be given to the lighting, costume, and set designers; the director, his assistants, and choreographers; and members of the stage management team, the master electrician, and the costume shop manager.

Chapter 8
Start "Propping"

"I can't wait to get started!" Start planning your prop-acquiring process. Put your budget amounts and your prop list in front of you and begin. What will you need to buy? Where will you find it? What do you need to rent or borrow, and whom can you call? Pull out the phone, phone book, and map and hop in the car — but make sure you have a plan of attack first.

Get Going!

It is believed that gathering the props for a show is in the blood of every prop master. As if you descended directly from the Great Chief Prop Man himself, born with powerfully intimidating and admirable prop-hunting instincts, it is assumed you arrived at the job knowing exactly which methods were the right ones for the sport of procuring props. Foraging for props might be the only part of the job that you have looked forward to all along, or maybe this is the part of the job you dread. Regardless, this chapter tells you how to tackle the hunt and prove that there has never been a prop master greater than you.

Making Priorities

Rehearsal Props

Before we go any further, it is important to know that the very first step in physically propping a show begins with providing rehearsal props. Some have joked that since you are providing rehearsal props in addition to the actual performance props, you're basically propping the show twice. Although this may seem like the truth sometimes, if you truly believe this, you're not doing your job correctly.

Gathering rehearsal props is an excellent jumping-off point for propping the show. Collecting rehearsal props will help you begin to organize your time, resources, and final propping approach.

While you are digging around in your prop stock or personal closets, you're discovering what potential performance props you have on hand. No step you take with supplying rehearsal props is done in vain. All of your hard work will take you a step closer to the end goal. More information on rehearsal props is explored in Chapter 9.

Create a "To-Do" List

A to-do list will organize your propping plan of attack. Propping a show is much more complex than being able to walk out the front door, turn around, and come back in again, your arms laden with props. It is a juggling act of "What do I do first?" and "How much time do I have left?" and "Where did my budget go?" mixed with "Where in the world am I going to find *that*?" Creating a to-do list in addition to the prop list will prepare you for the work ahead while helping you keep from forgetting something.

Set your prop list and cost breakdown list in front of you. Both of these documents that you worked so hard on constructing are the foundations for your propping plan — your to-do list. Using a legal pad, divide your to-do list into four separate pages, labeling each page with one of the following category headings: "To Borrow/Rent," "To Build/Make," "To Buy," "To Find/Pull." The descriptions of these categories are discussed later in this chapter.

Go through your prop list — prop by prop — and make an initial assignment concerning which page of your to-do list each prop will fall on. As you sort through each prop, remember to review the notes you took while reading the script, studying the designs, and conversing with the designer and director. These notes will have a major influence on which category a prop is assigned to. After you have gone through your prop list, do the same with your cost breakdown sheet. Change initial assignments around until your prop analysis places the item and its materials in the appropriate categories. Both the prop list and the cost breakdown sheet will bring to light many of the little building or shopping details about certain props you may not have already thought about.

If you are still having trouble figuring out how to divide the props into the categories, you can follow these general guidelines. (However, proceed with caution; these "rules" are certainly not tailored to your show and may have the potential to throw off your propping plan.)

- Set props and set dressing are frequently borrowed or rented. Buying these props is usually too costly.
- Props that are show specific, will suffer enormous amounts of abuse, need to function in a particular way, will be permanently altered, or must match designer drawings can be allocated to the "To Build" section.
- Materials for building props, consumable props, and things that are cheaper to buy than to rent or spend large amounts of time trying to find are classified as "To Buy."
- Props you intend "To Find/Pull" are items you already have in storage or know you'll find if you do some "dumpster diving."

Separating the props into different propping categories makes the to-do list easier to view and helps you focus on which props still require attention. You can look at your to-do list and immediately recall what props you still have to buy, what needs to be borrowed, and what you still have to build. Another perk for having a comprehensive to-do list is that it allows anyone assisting you to pick up where you left off in your propping process.

Remember to consider these factors:

- Do I have this prop in stock?
- Which props will be the hardest to acquire?
- Would buying a prop be cheaper than building it?
- Can set dressing or other props be placed on the back burner?
- Should obtaining hand props be my first priority?
- How is the prop used in the play?
- Will props or supplies need to be specially ordered?
- Do I still think my budget is big enough?
- Which projects can I assign to the prop crew? Will I need overhire personnel?

Of course, once you are embroiled in your prop hunting, your to-do list will change and evolve. It will get longer as information comes in from rehearsals. It will become shorter as you work hard to cross items off the list. It will get thrown out the window as your initial plan of attack becomes null and void. Props you

> **Remember that your to-do list will constantly change throughout the entire rehearsal process.**

thought could be borrowed will need to be bought. Props you thought you could buy will have to be rented. Props you spent days building will be completely cut from the show and new props will be needed to take their places. As long as you remain flexible to prop changes and fully understand that the to-do list will never be set in stone, all of your work will eventually be completed.

To Borrow/Rent: Acquiring From Someone Else

Borrowing and renting props is a great way to prop your show. Nine times out of ten there is someone or someplace else in the world that has exactly what you are looking for and doesn't mind if you use it. This is also a great way to promote your own company and production while meeting and creating contacts with like-minded theater lovers. Schools, area theaters, certain vendors or companies, private citizens, and even Grandma may let you borrow specific things for your production. As these people get to know you, they may allow you to borrow or rent bigger ticket items with special perks. They might even call on you for help with their own projects and needs. And thus, excellent working relationships can evolve.

To Borrow

The Merriam-Webster Dictionary defines "Borrow" as: "to take or receive something temporarily with the intent to return the same or an equivalent." Even if your prop budget allows you to buy the moon and a space station, part of the thrill of propping is seeking out what props or materials you can borrow from someone else free of charge.

Bartering

Depending on the policies of your theater, bartering with those from whom you borrow can produce great results. Some theaters will let prop masters offer free tickets to the show or advertisement space in the play program as bartering leverage. Great-Aunt Ethel may be more willing to let you borrow the crystal chandelier from her foyer in exchange for free tickets to the show you're working on. The owner of the local discount furniture retailer would gladly accept your offer of free advertising in exchange for lending you the rather expensive cherry presidential desk set that he can't seem to sell.

Thanking People

Thank those who have saved you a ton of time and money by lending their possessions to you and entrusting items to your care. A verbal thank you is a good start, but sending a genuine thank-you card or note on your company's letterhead is priceless. Thank-you notes will fashion you as a true professional and prove your gratitude. Recognizing the lender for their tremendously helpful deed through a program acknowledgment is wonderful as long as the marketing department agrees to the space in the program and the request is made before the program goes to the printer.

To Rent

From this same dictionary, *The Merriam-Webster*, the definition for "Rent" is: (noun) "money paid or due at intervals for the use of another's property," and (verb) "to take and hold under an agreement to pay rent." Essentially, renting is like borrowing because you do not intend to possess the item indefinitely. Unlike borrowing, however, when you rent you are paying a fee to the owner for the use of this item. Most major cities have prop rental houses, and some theaters and schools prefer to rent props rather than lend them. Before you make rental appointments, prepare a list of props you hope the organization will have.

Before you rent props, ask yourself these questions:

- Have I completely read and understood the terms of the rental agreement?
- Can I afford to buy the item at value if it is damaged while in my possession?
- Are the total rental costs cheaper than buying similar items somewhere else?
- Do I have enough money in my budget for this rental?
- Am I allowed to make alterations to the item?
- Have I provided the proper beginning and end dates for this rental?
- Before I commit to a rental and fees, am I sure this prop is what the director and designer are looking for?
- If I return the rented prop before the return date, will I have to pay the full rental fee?

113

Treat borrowed or rented props with special care!

Renting props should never feel like a life-or-death decision, but common sense may save you a ton of money in the end. Renting may save time and end a prop pursuit, but it is sometimes more costly than simply purchasing the props.

Renting and Borrowing Etiquette

Know the rules of being a courteous borrower and renter of theatrical properties. Whether you borrow or rent, remember that the prop is not yours. If props cannot be returned in the condition in which they were borrowed or rented, then they should be bought or built instead. Do not borrow something so valuable you could never afford to replace it in good faith. No one will lend or rent their things to you if you have shown that you cannot properly handle or safeguard their things. Your track record will precede you.

Own Up to Mistakes

Props do break sometimes. As much as we prop masters hate to think of such things, it does happen. Adding to the frustration of dealing with a broken performance prop is the knowledge the item does not belong to your company. Not only does this mean that you'll have to find a new prop, but it also means you'll have to tell the owner that something has happened to his property. Yes, you do need to tell him. A song and dance routine about how the prop was broken or whose fault it is does not matter. The best plan is to accept the fault as your own, alert the owner about what the damage is, and offer to repair the item as well as possible or have it professionally repaired.

Uphold Rental Agreement Conditions

If you have signed a rental agreement, then you follow the terms both parties agreed to when signing it. If props were borrowed or rented on good faith, then you could be vulnerable to whatever course of action the owner decides to take. Return the borrowed or rented props by the agreed-upon date. Failure to do so will result in more rental fees and poor marks on your professional reputation.

"Heads up. That's rented."

A good stage management team will understand the value of treating borrowed and rented items with care. Nine stage managers out of ten will do their utmost to help prevent props from becoming damaged or lost. Keep stage management informed with an updated list of rehearsal or performance props that are not owned by your company. Stage managers that have this information are more inclined to make sure you know of damages right away rather than having you discover them as you hand the prop back to the owner. Full information might nip a director's prop alteration notions in the bud before damage is done.

To Build: The Creative Side

To Build

Merriam-Webster claims that to "build" means: "1. to form by ordering and uniting materials, to bring into being or develop; 2. to produce or increase gradually." Sounds about right — a perfect definition for the theater's use of the word.

Build vs. Make

In technical theater, or theater production, we build things. If it can be built, then we want to build it. We build everything: sets, props, costumes, light cues, and sound cues. We build curtains, blocking, suit coats, and door units. We say, "I built that," "We just finished building the set," "The cues are built," and even use the term as a noun: "This whole production has been a crazy build." We never seem to *make* things in theater. We only *build* them.

Build vs. Buy

Long ago, it was less expensive to build things yourself than to buy them in the store. Nowadays, this isn't always the case. Raw materials that are available to the consumer are now rare and expensive. This doesn't bode well for theater technicians or theaters across the board. You have to weigh the budget and time pros and cons when you are faced with the choice between buy and build. However, there are certain prop elements that cannot be bought because they are specifically designed, leaving you no choice except to pay the fees and get the job done. Fabric, lumber, crafting supplies — you name it, it's costly.

On the upside of materials, there are things for sale that long ago didn't exist unless you built them. Items that were next to impossible to hunt down are much more available today. When your prop budget is large enough, sometimes buying the prop will prove to be more cost effective that building it. If you dream it, want it, feel it, you can buy it.

The Prop Build

The prop build incorporates any and all activities that alter, add onto, adhere, build, create, craft, destroy, dye, design, distress, fashion, figure out, fix, generate, mold, put together, reinforce, repair, and refinish props. Props that are very specific to the play (paper props, signs, special effects, etc.) or to the design (a farm wagon, bench, wall hanging, etc.) will need to be found and altered or built from scratch. Any prop that will suffer abuse as a result of the action of the play will need to be carefully reinforced or structurally crafted to withstand the blows. When it comes to antiques, sometime it's just easier to build new than to refinish or constantly repair something fragile. Props that have to function, look, weigh, or feel a certain way will also fall under the plans of the build.

Working with Designs

Either included with the set elevations or provided separately, the set designer will provide drawn-out plans for set props and hand props that play an important role in the show and have such an obscure description or function that they could never be found in the "real world." When you build something from a design, it's important to follow the measurements and details that are indicated in the drawings. Deviation from the designs should only occur if approved by the designer; otherwise, the prop may wind up being too big to serve its purpose.

Using Ingenuity

Building props can be a lot of fun. This is the time when the prop master can demonstrate his many prop crafting talents or have a rare learning opportunity. Playing around with "what works" and "what doesn't" when it comes to techniques and materials can be both exasperating and exhilarating. Discovering that a golf ball works as a great middle piece for a curtain rod finial will make you look like a genius *and* save money. Depending on the project, junk that is lying around the shop or old props marked for the trash pile may find a new life and be recycled into something perfect for the show.

Tricks for Tackling "Creator's Block"

Building a prop from scratch with no design is next to impossible when you are out of ideas on how to go about it. When you're stuck, you can study similar objects that already exist. If you need to build a specific item, research the existing construction of similar things. If your prop never existed to begin with and there is no research to be found, then sit back, close your eyes, and let your creative juices flow:

- Create a mental image of the finished product.
- While it's still in your mind, scrutinize every part of the image. Zero in on every detail.
- Start breaking apart the image. If you were to invent this item and patent it, how would the parts connect? What kind of "innards" would it have?
- Envision every material, real-life object, and building supply that you can think of that could replicate or be fashioned into the various parts of the object in your mind.

If this process doesn't work, go ask your boss or a co-worker for ideas.

To Buy: Purchasing Props

I believe it can be safely assumed that all of us know what "to buy" means in prop land. But just to be sure, the dictionary definition of "buy" is: "to obtain for a price; to purchase." What you can buy depends on your budget. Perhaps your budget is not very large. How do you get all of the props and materials you need to buy? Consult your cost breakdown sheet — you've already done the hard work. Minding the cost breakdown will help keep you within budget.

Budget-Saving Store Ideas

Antique Stores
Resale/Thrift Stores
Yard Sales
Auctions
Dollar Stores
Craft Stores
Hardware Stores
Discount Retail Stores

Buying Tips

- Spend time bargain hunting.
- Shy away from impulse shopping and take your time.
- Choose generic knock offs instead of brand names.
- Favor used items over brand new things.

The typical restrictions which prohibit you from shopping at top-dollar stores are budget and common sense. Can you imagine what your supervisor would say if you blew your entire $500 materials budget on one set of curtains at the department store? Be proactive and make that budget stretch. Shop at places that are tailored to fit your budget requirements. With the aid of the Internet, a phone book, phone, and a map, you'll discover great budget-saving places to shop.

Can It Be Returned?

The only caveat I can offer when shopping at yard sales, auctions, and some antique and resale/thrift stores is that most things cannot be returned for a refund or exchange if the props don't wind up working for your production. Think about your budget and your purchases carefully before you give in to the buying impulse. There are worse things you can do than spend your entire budget on props that cannot be used for the show, but I can't think of any.

In the interest of time and resources, sometimes you have to take a risk and go with your gut feeling. You may come across a great deal on the perfect prop, and time may prohibit you from seeking everyone's opinion. Just be sure that what you are buying will be the prop you can use.

To Find/Pull Props

To Find

To "find," according to *Merriam-Webster*, means: "(verb) 1. to meet with either by chance or by searching. 2. to obtain by effort or management." Appropriating all props takes effort and management. Coming across something you need for the show that is free, that does not belong to anyone, that is either the perfect prop or the perfect material to create the perfect prop, can be called *the perfect find*.

Other good places to find props may not be the places you normally frequent. Dumpster diving, a popular term for trash digging, while dangerous and in some places illegal, has been known to produce some great props. The phrase "one man's trash is another man's treasure" is the motto of the prop master.

Great places for finding or pulling props

Prop Storage
Closets of Friends and Family
Corners in the Theater Building
Dumpsters
Friendly Theaters and Schools
Board Members' Basements

To Pull

Prop storage or stock is an excellent place to find props. Props you pulled for rehearsal that also have show potential can be a fantastic find. A prop pulled from stock might possess the promise of morphing into a better or worse version of itself or into something completely different. With the help of altering ingenuity and elbow grease, that simple prop from stock could be transformed into a magnificent thingamabob. Of course, you don't want to permanently modify your valuable stock pieces or any pieces that you like to use on a regular basis.

Share the Wealth

Do Not Prop Alone

Your personal safety is important. Use the buddy system if you need to go traipsing around in less-than-ideal environments. It never hurts to have an extra set of muscles to help you load the cast-iron, claw-footed tub into the back of the van. Don't go it alone. You don't ever want to find yourself in a scary, dangerous, or physically harmful situation. Props aren't worth that much. Think ahead and share the propping fun: Bring a friend and some street smarts on your adventures.

You Are Not Alone

Don't forget to share the wealth and bounty of your prop hunt. When you are out and about, assessing the options within the propping environment, present your leads and findings to the appropriate guest artists and production department heads. Share pictures of the props you come across and relay size information as well. A prop that plays an important role in the show requires confirmation that it is the right prop for the job.

You are part of the decision-making process, and your thoughts, advice, and knowledge will be just as important as the ideas of the guest artists. You are not propping any show alone. You have a support group of directors and designers who rely on you to do your job well and want you to succeed. These same people want to be active in the process of realizing the concept and design. They encourage a cooperative team effort. Share the wealth — the wealth of information, the wealth of projects, and the wealth of concerns. Share what you've found. Ask for opinions, ask for answers, ask for help, take advice, and raise your red flag. Please remember that in this collaborative art form, you are not alone.

Chapter 9
Rehearsals and Performances

"They want to make changes to all the props I supplied for rehearsals. Who do they think they are?" Theater is an ever-changing, creative process. Prop change requests come down the line until opening night, and it is usually stage management that gets to deliver the news. Be prepared and enter into the rehearsal, tech, and performance processes with a calm attitude and a brave smile.

Daily Rehearsal Period

By the time the rehearsal process begins, prop work should be in full swing. The rehearsal process provides directors with the time and opportunity to block and work with the actors. Stage managers use this opportunity to study and absorb every aspect of the entire show. Production departments and designers continue to get all the technical elements together. Production meetings frequently crop up, and there is excitement in the air as deadlines draw near.

Rehearsal Props

Actors use daily rehearsal time to learn their lines and become familiar with the design of the set and the props that fill the space. In order for actors to familiarize themselves with their future stage surroundings during rehearsals, they need to rehearse with props. A rehearsal prop is like a "stand-in" prop, something that represents what the performance prop will

> **Rehearsal props give the actors a chance to practice their blocking and actions.**

look like. Rehearsal props need to be very similar to the performance prop in size and function, but can be found items, pulled from stock or quickly crafted.

In the director's and actors' ideal world, the props you provide for rehearsals would be the performance props, perfect and complete in every way. (And that would be a prop master's dream, too.) However, this is rarely the case. The first props you need to provide are all rehearsal props that play a key role in the action. These are usually the hand and set props. Set dressing should be included if it will affect actor blocking. As long as there are no serious concerns for the safety of the props, rehearsal props can also be the performance props. Sometimes, a prop intended solely for rehearsal will be so adored by the creative team that it will receive performance prop status. This is great news — another prop to cross off your to-do list.

If you have the performance prop, introduce it into rehearsal and replace the rehearsal prop as soon as possible. The longer the actor has to work with her props, the more time she will have to adjust to them and the better she will like them. Depending on the performer, sometimes the slightest adjustment or difference in a prop can throw a cog in the works. The faster you exchange rehearsal props with performance props during the rehearsal process, the happier your actor friends will be.

Stage managers, directors, and actors prefer to have rehearsal props in the rehearsal room ready for use during the first few days of rehearsal. In professional theater, most actors like to start working with props at the start of blocking rehearsals. The deadline for providing initial rehearsal props should be discussed with the director and stage manager well before rehearsals begin.

There are going to be times when you may not be able to provide a specific rehearsal prop for an actor to use right away. It does happen. Sometimes the prop you need is next to impossible to find, has to be specially ordered, or must be built, and there isn't time or money to spend on creating a rehearsal version when resources are better spent procuring the performance prop. When cases like these occur, spend a little time giving everyone in rehearsal a clear understanding of what you are looking for or plan to build and explain why they won't see it in the rehearsal room right away. Provide stage management and directors with research pictures, drawings, and model pieces of what they can expect from the future performance prop.

Organized Rehearsal Props

The rehearsal hall should never become cluttered with rehearsal props. Keeping rehearsal props organized helps create a calm and inviting work environment. Most likely, stage management will make it their business to organize the hand props once they arrive to rehearsal. However, if they fail to do so, step up to the plate. Props strewn about the room can create mental chaos for the guest artists who have a lot more to worry about than what they're stepping on. Organized rehearsal props are less likely to break, easy to find, easy to put back, and easy to repair or replace with performance props.

Every prop brought to rehearsal should have a designated place. Set props and set dressings necessary to rehearsals should be placed in the rehearsal space in the position indicated by the ground plan or other set design information. It is possible that the rehearsal space is not as large as the stage, so adjustments to furniture placement should be made accordingly. Tables or shelves should be set up in the areas of the room dubbing as wings of the stage. Hand props should be nicely displayed on the shelves for easy access.

Props should be brought into the rehearsal hall only when rehearsal is not taking place. Allow yourself enough time to carry in, unload, and set up props in designated spots before rehearsal begins for the day. Dropping props off after rehearsal is over or during break times also works. Unless requested to do so by the director or stage management, never interrupt rehearsal with a prop drop or conversation.

Meet with stage management often to discuss prop needs. In-person meetings present the perfect opportunity to pass along special prop information, such as which props are rented or need special care, how trick props work, which of the rehearsal props will be the actual performance props, etc. Props may break or get damaged during rehearsal. This is the risk all prop masters take. Providing stage management with a list of rented or borrowed props will not insure the items against damage but will inform the stage management team of their limited uses.

Rehearsal Reports

A rehearsal report is an account of all show-related discussions generated throughout a rehearsal day. Prepared daily by the stage manager, these reports contain information concerning what scenes were rehearsed that day, how long each scene is running, the next day's schedule, and, most importantly, notes that affect the production departments. The rehearsal report is the primary way information is distributed from the rehearsal to all theater departments and guest artists. A standard rehearsal report in e-mail form can be seen in Figure 9.1.

Prop Master

From:	Stage Manager
Sent:	Wednesday, May 6
To:	Theater Staff and Artists
Subject:	Title of Production Rehearsal Report

Rehearsal Report #12
Wednesday May 6th

Tomorrow's Schedule
12pm Record Newscaster
1pm Rehearse Act 1
1pm Costume Fitting w/ Steve
2:30pm Fitting with Chris
3:15 Break
3:30 Designer Run-through

Announcements
Thank you to Jose for running lines with Chris
Production Meeting Friday @ 5pm

Prop Notes
- Frank's letter should be smaller—4" x 6"
- Add plastic cup of water for George
- Please fix the armchair. The seat sags and joints are loose
- Add 2 trumpets—they will be played by Frank and George
- Megan does not want toothpaste, just a toothbrush
- The coffee table was tipped over in the fight rehearsal.
- Thanks for all the new props!

Set Notes
- The front door will be slammed 3 times in sc. 1
- Please reinforce down SL wall for fight
- Thanks for the rehearsal stairs

Costume Notes
- Megan crawls on stage in Act 1 skirt

Light Notes
None
Sound Notes
None

Thank you, everyone!
Stage Manager

Figure 9.1

Pertinent Information

Prop masters garner a good portion of production information from rehearsal reports. Rehearsal reports give you an inside look into what is happening in rehearsal. The props notes section is ordinarily filled with thoughts, comments, requests, notices, reminders, needs, changes, and additions from the director and actors. Announcement alerts offer a future "heads up" for impending photo calls, meetings, or other events. The daily rehearsal schedule can help you plan your own schedule for the next day. If you need to take props to the rehearsal space, pick up props that need repair, or grab a moment to speak with the director or stage manager, you have a good idea when it is appropriate to do so.

Frequently, a note in another department's section of the rehearsal report will influence your department's work. For example, if there is a set note that states the front door will be slammed very hard on an actor's entrance, you will know to reinforce the rigging for any set dressing attached to these flats so nothing will fall during a performance.

Occasionally, a stage manager, just like any other human, is bound to make an error, and it is not uncommon to see a prop note written in another department's section. A common example of this is when costume props are used. Oftentimes, stage management doesn't know which department has supplied what, and the rehearsal notes may reflect this small confusion. By reading all the notes in the rehearsal report you can catch these minor mistakes before the costume shop fills the request and dulls the blade on the rented dagger Hamlet hides in his boot.

Prop Use and Abuse

The rehearsal report will give you a good sense of how well the props you've already supplied are working. You may receive notes on what you thought was a perfect performance prop. According to the needs of rehearsal, this perfect prop may not work well for the production if even for the simple the reason that it is too big, too small, or just not right. After a little investigation to determine what the ideal prop really is, you will be better equipped to hunt down something that fits the bill.

Rehearsal reports will also alert you about the way your props are being used. You may already know that the chef stands on the armchair, but did you know that during the argument scene between the mother and son the director would block the actors to joust with a table lamp and a dining chair? Sometimes the only indication of such blocking comes from the rehearsal report. These notes give you a chance to "raise your red flag" if you are concerned about the welfare of your props and time to exchange the truly antique lamp with a reinforced plastic replica.

Caring About Actors

Actors are people, too. And just like you and me, they have a hard job. While they are busy assuming the mentality and personality of another person for hours on end, they still have to retain a part of themselves in order to remember their blocking, their lines, and all the other techniques expected from the profession. It's draining work, and actors are bound to get cranky from time to time, just like the rest of us. And, just like the rest of us, actors can get frustrated if the tools of their trade don't fit their needs or don't function as expected. And, like you and me, actors will bleed if pricked or poked.

The stage manager will be the first to tell you if a prop poses a hazard to an actor. I have had to re-sand table edges that, to me, were smooth to begin with; pull forgotten staples that I didn't catch when finishing a project; and grind down the tips of screws that were poking through an upholstered chair because actors unearthed these threats. The prop master is also human and certain to make errors, yet diligence should not be set aside when it comes to actor/prop safety. Not meant to be a demeaning comment, just an honest one: actors sometimes have the sensitivity of the princess and her pea. They are bound to find a hazard you may not have noticed. As if commanded by a magnetic force, actors are drawn to potential danger. If you accidentally leave a pin in the upholstery, the underside of a table un-sanded, or a knife blade a little too sharp, actors will discover this oversight. When you get notes about these difficulties, rectify the situation immediately.

When you are propping, assume the role of an actor. Take extra measures to find the forgotten staples and address the small hazards or inconveniences before the actor does. When discussing prop needs with actors, imagine yourself in their shoes. Fulfill their requests when possible and as soon as possible. The props you lovingly provide for the show are ultimately more important to the actor than they are to you. Once a show is open, you will move on to the next props project while the actor must faithfully stick with the job at hand. Care about your actors.

Responding to Rehearsal Reports

Sometimes the sheer volume of prop notes coming from rehearsals can be daunting and frustrating, especially when the changes, the questions, the requests, and the prop adds seem to create another day or two of work on top of your already enormous work list. However, ignoring these notes won't make them go away, even if that is your greatest wish.

Receiving rehearsal notes is all a part of the job and should be considered as another project that needs to be tackled. At the start of your workday, build in time for reading and responding to the daily rehearsal reports. Transfer prop additions or changes to your prop list and to-do list. During this time, determine if any of the new prop requests are a priority. Respond to stage management and answer any questions presented to your department. Provide them with an estimated day and time when you think some notes might be accomplished and brought to rehearsal so they can rest assured that you are already working on them.

Take this time to clarify any questions you might have for stage management about notes which are vague or need more detail. No matter how large or small, prop details are important. For example, a new note mentions "the actors will now be drinking tea and could you bring some to rehearsal." You'd be "happy to comply," you reply to stage management, if they will tell you "what kind of tea is expected and how will it be served?" Potential problems could arise if you don't ask for details. Time and money could be wasted supplying the wrong prop, and that can be frustrating to both parties. With a simple request of tea for rehearsal, the specifics about this new prop add were not provided. Did stage management mean for the tea to be hot or iced, sweetened or unsweetened, tea bags or dry mix, decaf or regular, herbal or plain? How will the tea be served: glass or plastic, bottles or cans, tray and pitcher, how much, how many? When? Where? What?! Why?! (Yep. Sometimes propping a show can feel this ludicrous. But fun, remember. Fun!)

Keep an Eye on Your Budget

Before promising to fulfill a new prop request for the moon, check your budget again. Will the changes, additions, or requests fit into your budget? Can you afford to buy the moon, or will you have to break the news to rehearsal that the moon is too expensive — would something else suffice? It is not the job of the director and stage management to think about your budget limits when they create and send off their notes. Find out how important having the moon is to members of rehearsal. If they can't live without it, this might be a prop for which you use your saved budget money. If you are truly concerned about your budget, raise that red flag.

Production Meetings and Attending Rehearsals

With your prop bible in hand, you can attend production meetings with confidence. Production meetings provide a face-to-face opportunity to discuss schedules and production concerns with all production team members. These meetings give you the chance to talk directly with the director and set designer and really nail down prop specifics, get answers to questions you have, solve problems, ease concerns, etc. Production meetings are not optional. If you cannot attend the meeting or may be late, tell your supervisor and stage manager as soon as you know. If you do need to miss a meeting, send someone in your place who can represent the prop department and make sure you find out what important information you missed.

Attending a rehearsal or two will let you see the progress of the show before the rehearsal process goes into tech. Watching rehearsals is the best way to clear up any prop questions or confusion you might have. You can see for yourself just how your props are being used (or abused). Any concerns you have after watching rehearsal will be addressed in time for the start of tech.

Learning When to Say "No"

There is a time in the production process when the prop master may put a polite yet firm end to the prop requests. A prop request deadline serves as an end date for any major prop additions or alterations and usually falls a few days before the start of technical rehearsals. Knowing when to provide a prop request deadline and how to correctly convey "enough is enough" varies depending on the preferences of the prop master. Some prop masters prefer these deadlines to be part of the regular production calendar deadlines. Others will provide stage management with an end date on a case-by-case basis determined by resource availability and production circumstances. It must be said that a prop request deadline is only meant as a way to let the prop department catch up with the demands of the production and ensure that all props previously listed or requested will be provided by the time technical rehearsals begin. No doubt, notes will still trickle in from rehearsal after the deadline no matter how hard everyone is trying to stand by your request.

Prop Load-In

Prop load-in occurs the day before tech rehearsals begin and is the allotted time period when all of the performance props are brought to the stage and loaded in to their appropriate places within the physical set. Prop load-in is usually scheduled during a time of the day when it is safe to permanently steal away all of the performance props the actors have been using. To the stage they go!

The prop master organizes load-in specifics ahead of time. The transportable tool kit makes its appearance, performance props and set dressing not needed in the rehearsal hall are finally brought to the stage, stage time is coordinated with other production departments (who are also finishing up their own load-in schedules), and a crew of muscle is amassed for the big move to the stage.

Organizing Props On-stage and Backstage

When it comes to putting hand props and set props in their proper places, the stage management team is your best reference. Since they are the experts on all things pertaining to the performance, they will know where every hand or set prop will need to be at the start of every performance. Because they have been tracking the whereabouts of the props throughout the show, they will also know where the props end up after each scene and act. If you have a question while loading in, stage management can most likely answer it.

Prop Tables

The stage management team will set up prop tables as necessary in backstage areas. Prop tables (Figure 9.2) organize and display hand props that start the show offstage, or will rest offstage at some point during the performance. These tables or

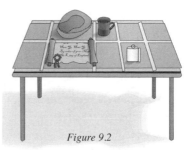

Figure 9.2

shelves are placed in an area backstage that is accessible yet out of harm's way. I have seen many prop tables destroyed during a scene change because they were set up in the path of set pieces. I have also witnessed an actor accidentally charge into a prop table during a hurried exit off of a well-lit stage into the pitch-blackness of backstage.

Prop tables are covered with a fixed layer of brown craft paper (white paper bounces too much stage light). The table is divided into a grid of squares or sections with masking tape or marker. The sections help define a special space in which each prop will reside, while trying to maximize the number of spaces on each table. Use a marker to label each space with the name of the prop that occupies it. Sometimes stage management will lay props on the paper and create the prop's special spot by outlining the prop in permanent marker. This method is fine unless props are cut from the show or change in shape or size.

A well-lit prop table is a must. The backstage areas are extremely dark. The actor who cannot see a prop table and grabs the butcher knife instead of the flowers will be in for an awful surprise on-stage. Nearly all theaters are equipped with clip lights or other special backstage lights that use low-watt light bulbs covered with blue gel to minimize light spill on-stage. These lights are the perfect addition to prop tables and will prevent confusion.

Food props and replacements for other consumable props are brought into the theater space during load-in and handed over to stage management. If food is to be prepared a certain way, spend time showing the task to the member of stage management who is assigned to this duty. Any other operating or care instructions you have for particular props should be shared with stage management at this time and throughout tech when possible.

Dressing the Set

Dressing the set is the part of prop load-in which can be fun and rewarding. Finally, weeks of prop work are brought together for the first time. Set dressing (the props that embellish the set to add those perfect finishing touches) is installed and displayed on the set. All dressing decisions are either made or approved by the set designer, who is usually actively involved in this part of the prop process. Dressing the set is also fun for the designer. Seeing his design realized on-stage with all the details is a great reward for months of creative labor. Some words of advice: Never be without a notepad and pen when you are in the presence of the designer.

Types of Set Dressing Activities

- Setting props in place according to the designs or action of the play.
- Hanging picture frames, shelving, and other wall dressing.
- Installing blinds and window treatments.
- Installing and wiring lighting practicals.
- Filling floor space and/or furniture surfaces with set dressing.
- Securing props to the set.

A popular and common analogy prop masters use for describing this part of the work to non-theater people compares dressing the set to moving into a new home. No matter how majestic and intricate the design, a box set or home would seem bare and empty without furniture and all the things used for decorating surfaces or hanging on walls. Similar to moving, dressing the set is the act of moving the furniture into the space and finding a home for all the props within the confines of the walls.

In theater, as opposed to real life, set props have assigned positions on the stage. After weeks of rehearsal, actors anticipate that the set elements and prop placements will be approximately the same on-stage as they were in rehearsal. This is something to keep in mind when dressing the set. All-new set dressing should not be placed on-stage where it will be in the way of the actors' blocking and affect the rehearsed traffic patterns. If the show you are working on has a lot of set dressing that the actors will have to maneuver around, supply these props to rehearsal ahead of time. If some dressing is not indicated on the ground plan, ask the set designer and director where exact placement should be. Few actors are graceful enough to spontaneously leap over the new pile of junk in their way in the midst of a dramatic soliloquy. Care for your actors.

Securing Props to Spaces

Except for hand props, set props and dressing are often temporarily attached or adhered to the surfaces on which they rest or lean on-stage — the floor, walls, windows, shelves, tables, etc. Scene shifts and actor movements could cause a fatal mishap to an unsecured prop and in turn harm the actor or disrupt the action. Unsecured props sometimes upstage actors.

Here are two true stories: A prop traveling on a wagon (rolling platform) during a scene shift threw itself onto the stage floor. Crashing into bits upon landing, the "accident" made the scene shift stop, the audience gasp, and the actors practice their improvisation skills. A rug that had been rolled up in storage for years preferred to keep its edges curled when laid flat on-stage. Almost as if planned, the rug's edges caught the toes of an unsuspecting actor. The actor tripped. The rest is history. Only *you* can prevent these tragedies from occurring.

What props should be secured:

- All props that face even the remotest possibility of being knocked over or off of a surface — picture frames, lamps, knickknacks, coat racks, etc.
- Set props or set dressing that have a tendency to slide or move out of place — rugs, sofas, tables, chairs, etc.
- All things which hang — lighting fixtures, window treatments, shower curtain rods, picture frames, signs, etc.

Methods and products for temporarily yet effectively securing props to surfaces:

- **Mortite®:** A brand name for gray or brown putty-like weather-strip or caulking cord that stays malleable for a long time. Prop masters use pieces of this to fix smaller props to surfaces. Mortite® is sticky and easily smashed in between the object and the surface. It is removable but may leave a tiny bit of residue.
- **Staple Gun:** Staples for this gun come in many lengths, from a quarter inch to over a half inch long. Fabrics, carpets, cardboard, and paper are best attached to hard surfaces with the staple gun. This is the best way to secure curled rug edges. Staples are removable, but leave small holes in the surfaces.

- **Screws:** Using screws for props that would normally require screws for installation (light fixtures, curtain rods, wall shelves) is usually the best choice. You may prefer to use screws to hang picture frames and metal signs because screws are easier to place and remove than nails. Sometimes the legs of set and dressing props will need to be attached to platforms or other flooring. Oftentimes, long screws pre-drilled at an angle through the upstage or offstage legs and into the flooring can be enough to stabilize large set props. Corner irons attached to the leg and the flooring provide more support, but might be seen by the audience. Screws are removable but leave large holes in surfaces
- **Tie Line:** Slightly stiff, black-colored, thin, cotton rope; tie line has limitless purposes and is used mostly by the set and electrics departments. Just a little bit of tie line, and the prop master becomes MacGyver. Tie line is removable when untied.
- **Gaffer Tape:** Gaffer tape is a strong, cotton-cloth, adhesive tape used as a multi-purpose tool or material. In a pinch, "gaff" tape can be used to hold props in place or as a seam cover to prevent light leaks. Gaff tape is removable but strong enough to pull paint, fibers, and top layers of veneer from surfaces.

The method you use to secure your props should take into account several factors:
- Is the prop rented? What am I allowed to do to it?
- Am I willing to sacrifice value for safety?
- Which method best serves the show's needs?

If you actually *want* set props or dressing to slide or glide across surfaces, or to keep the bottom of props from scratching surfaces, plastic or felt furniture glides will do the trick.

Hiding the Uglies

As you dress the set, you'll discover things you want to keep the audience from noticing. From a small scratch in the furniture to obvious theater-only methods, audience members are fascinated by being able to view the "magic" behind the magic, and can be madly distracted by obvious errors and inattention to detail.

Before the doors are opened to the public and after prop placement is locked in, go around the stage and hide the uglies. Walk around the theater house and look at your props from the audience's view. Make note of props or problems that could be the least bit distracting. Of course, you want the audience to marvel at your props, but the props should stay out of the negative limelight whenever possible. Addressing these minor details really makes the set look tight, purposeful, and intentional.

Common theater uglies the prop master can control:

- Anything you see that needs polishing, dusting, or fixing; make note and take care of it.
- Prop electrical cords that bunch on the floor or lead to nowhere should be "dressed," meaning that the excess should be neatly bundled and hidden behind other props if possible.
- Props that shine too brilliantly or reflect too much light like picture frame glass, mirrors, and metals, should be toned down.
- Extra globs of Mortite® should be removed from surfaces.
- Screws securing props to the stage should not be visible to the audience.
- Loose fabric threads should be clipped from draperies, slip covers, etc.
- Tablecloths and other fabrics visible to the audience should be ironed or steamed.
- Furniture is sometimes placed at just the right angle for the audience to have a clear view of the piece's backside. Most furniture backsides are not pretty. Correct the look with a new piece of wood or a nicely fashioned solid curtain of dark or black fabric.
- Unless it is part of the design, there should be no raw wood on the set. Either stain it, paint it the color it should be, or paint it black (as long as that won't make it stand out more).
- Sometimes audience members in the first few rows of the house can glimpse the undersides of set props and the audience in the balconies can see the tops of tall props or even inside set props.
- Pad and tape screw tips that may stick through to the backstage side of flats.

Alerting Stage Management of Prop Changes

After prop load-in, anytime you make an adjustment to a prop, add a prop of any kind, take away a prop, or change prop placement, stage management must be notified. Surprise changes in the appearance of any part of the set are rarely welcome. Stage management needs to have time to pass your notes along to crew members or actors. Sharing this prop information is an act of courtesy.

Tech Rehearsals

Technical rehearsals, also known as "tech" or "tech week," are rehearsals leading up to opening night when all of the technical production elements and actors come together on-stage to create a solid visual performance. Cue by cue, the entire show is built, rehearsed, and re-rehearsed during the tech process. Light cues, sound cues, quick changes, scene changes, entrances, exits, actor lines, and special effects all have to be integrated and perfected.

The designers are "in residence" during tech, meaning that they watch every minute of the tech rehearsals. Lighting and sound designers madly build and modify their cues, and the set and costume designers take notes on what elements of their designs need adjustments, making themselves available to help solve design-related crises.

Tech is a time of high energy with alternating moments of concentrated stress and joyful lightheartedness. The entire production team comes together for the experience of very long work hours for several days. For the prop department, it is the final push.

The First Deadline

The first day of tech is the official deadline for having every performance prop done and ready to go. Depending on the amount of props vs. time and extra hands, tech could be considered the "first" deadline. If you have reached the start of tech with 90% of the show propped, and the remaining 10% is just set dressing and minor prop needs, then you are still on track.

You should be concerned if you have not yet procured the performance set and hand props. Props the actors use and major pieces of set dressing that define the play's environment are the most important props to have at the start of tech.

Actors are not the only ones disturbed if performance props are not ready by tech. Props have a major role in the design of the lights. Dark colored props will absorb stage light, and props lighter in color will bounce the light back. These factors change the intensity of each light and may have a bearing on what colors of gels are needed. Lighting designers determine how they will focus many of their lighting instruments based on the placement and size of props. Missing props impede the light designer's work.

The stage crew has a harder time rehearsing scene changes if props are absent from the stage. Scene changes are not just about changing set pieces; many scene changes are sometimes just prop changes. The director and set designer also need to view the full picture of the set during tech as they gain a sense of what elements of the design may need to be changed. The director, especially, has too much on his mind during tech to be responsible for remembering that an armoire will fill the enormous hole of space on stage right.

If you find yourself not ready for tech, you did not raise your red flag enough during the propping process. However, it is too late for hindsight, so find your supervisor, explain your predicament, follow his advice, and beg your best friend for propping help. Just get the show done!

Attending Tech Rehearsals

Tech Hours

In professional regional theater, tech rehearsals can run anywhere from six hours to a scheduled twelve-hour day with one two-hour break. The tech schedules are determined by theater managers in accordance with union rules and laws. A prop master's tech day could wind up being much longer than the scheduled rehearsal period. Depending on what's left on the to-do list, the prop crew might arrive at the theater a few hours before rehearsal begins and leave a few hours later. While the stage is being used for tech rehearsal time, actual prop, set, light, and sound work is prohibited, unless deemed necessary by the rehearsal powers-that-be. So, a twelve-hour rehearsal day may actually turn into a sixteen-plus hour workday for the prop master with only six of those sixteen hours allowed on set.

135

This is typical for tech. Expect long hours. Expect to be tired. If you expect these factors, then you'll accept them and not be bothered by them, and you'll be less likely to complain and annoy other team members who are in the same boat as you. And if you are expecting a long day, you'll be very pleasantly surprised if the director and designers decide to end tech rehearsal early one day.

Watching Rehearsal

It is helpful if the prop master can sit and watch tech rehearsals prepared to record any notes and prop concerns that pop up as production kinks are being worked out. However, it is not always possible for the prop master to spend the entire day in rehearsal, especially if there is still work to be done and props to be found.

If you have a staff of prop artisans working with you, delegate the projects so you can be free to watch rehearsals. If you are a department of one, your time would be better served getting the work done so the actors can work with the props. Make sure your absence is okay with those in rehearsal (production manager, director, stage manager, and set designer). Tell them where you plan to be, when you plan to return, and how they can contact you.

Run-throughs are a part of the tech rehearsal process that you don't want to miss. A tech run-through is when the actors, stage crew, stage manager, and board operators practice rehearsing the entire show from beginning to end, incorporating all of the new cues and show responsibilities. Watching these rehearsals gives you another chance to actually witness how the props are used in the show and take notes on prop changes.

Tech Notes

At the end of every technical rehearsal and preview performance, the production team is called together for a notes session to go over the events of the rehearsal day and discuss what worked, what didn't, and what needs to be changed — pronto. During notes sessions, the prop master will receive the prop remarks directly from the set designer, director, and stage manager. Add these prop notes to the prop list and to-do lists.

Making Changes

The prop notes derived from notes sessions should be taken care of as soon as possible. As you get farther into tech, the time you have to procure or alter a prop and the time the actor has to work with the new prop becomes less and less. Crossing these notes off your list may mean staying later or coming in much earlier to work than normal. Getting the notes done becomes imperative. Never risk your health or safety due to work hours, but do make some sacrifices in the effort to meet work deadlines when necessary.

Once again, if time or budget is a serious factor prohibiting you from fulfilling the note requests, raise the red flag. Keep sharing your realistic concerns if you have them. And, as always, alert stage management regarding any prop changes or notes you have completed.

Performances

Once opening night is celebrated, prop notes from the director and designer will cease, with the exception of the notes that show up in the stage manager's performance reports. In notes similar to rehearsal reports, the stage manager reviews each performance and includes any maintenance or replacement notes for the various departments. Prop performance notes are rare and are usually fairly easy fixes. Although the show is open, your prop work is never done. But, at least your preliminary props list is now finalized.

Prop Safety

Protecting props from blocking abuse and protecting actors from attack props has already been discussed. But what about keeping props safe from a curious individual?

Curiosity Killed the ...

Props are cool. No matter what kind of show is being produced, the props always draw the curious. Prop tables and props placed on set are attractive displays that people want to touch. Every theater employee, designer, director, and actor is guilty of breaking an important rule of theater: Do not touch someone else's props. The reason for this rule? All too often, props are picked up from one place and set down in another. This simple action is enough to make the stage manager have an anxiety attack while trying to hunt down the missing prop.

A common practice adopted by actors and stage management, in response to the curious who misplace other people's things, is to have a prop check before each performance. Stage management works on their preset duties making sure each prop is accounted for and in its proper place. Actors stroll through the set looking for each prop they work with during the show, double checking prop placement, and making sure props still work properly.

Locking Up Valuables

How do you keep a full stage of props and a backstage prop tables safe? Some theaters can lock up their auditoriums to prevent anyone not affiliated with the production from entering. Other theaters require all props not screwed to the set to be stripped from the set and prop tables and locked up in closets or storage areas in close proximity to the stage. Other theater companies operate on trust, locking away only extremely valuable props or weapons. The prop master should play a key role in determining which props need to be locked away after every performance. Don't hesitate to speak up if you want certain props locked up, and work to ensure that your requests are met.

Prop Maintenance

Once the production goes into tech, the finished performance props become the official responsibility of stage management, who will perform small maintenance repairs to props when needed and keep track of prop whereabouts and back-up supplies. All other responsibilities may fall on your shoulders, depending on the structure of your theater. The stage manager will alert you when prop maintenance is needed at any time during the run of the show. Performance prop maintenance includes:

- Food preparation
- Resetting effects
- Repairing props
- Replenishing consumables

Co-Productions

A co-production is the opportunity for two theater companies to produce the exact same show twice. Usually one theater will physically host the rehearsal processes and build of the show and will be the first theater to have a run of performances before the show is carefully struck and trucked over to the co-producing company's space where it will be performed for several more weeks. One of the benefits of co-producing is that both theaters will share the costs of building and rehearsing a production. Most of the time, co-productions are formed with theaters that reside at least an hour's drive from each other.

If you are the prop master at the theater that is building the show, you will follow all of your normal propping processes up through the performances. Before the show closes, spend some time putting together a packet of prop materials to give to the co-producing theater. Pictures of the set and props, the prop list, and a spreadsheet indicating where each numbered prop is placed should be a part of the packet. Whatever else you can do to help the other theater recreate the set once it is in their space will be much appreciated.

Strike of a co-production takes more planning than an average strike. Boxes and packaging materials should be supplied. Props should be packaged with other props that share the same stage space. As directed, the other theater will return any props that you wish them to after their strike. Any props you rented or borrowed for the show should be returned to you so you may then promptly return them to the issuing individual or organization.

Strike

Strike is the period of time when the theater's production personnel strip the stage of technical elements used in the most recent production. Strike takes place after the closing performance of each production, either immediately following the last performance or within the following few days. The prop master is in charge of gathering help for the prop side of strike. Armed with the transportable tool kit, several screw guns, and lots of boxes, milk crates, and laundry baskets, the prop strike crew is ready to go into action.

Coordinating Strike Stage Activities

A few days before strike, coordinate the activities and needs for prop strike with the strike plans of the technical director and master electrician. Sometimes prop and electric strikes will begin an hour or two before members of the set department show up. This is usually enough time for the majority of the props to be removed from the entire set. Discuss where props can be stored at the theater so they won't be in others' way until they can be taken to their proper home. If a company vehicle is shared during strike, double check which department will use it first and for how long. Most importantly, remember to work safely. Sometimes less care and more bravado is demonstrated at strike. Remember that the props and set pieces are just as heavy and dangerous at strike as they were during load-in.

Returning Props

Rented and Borrowed Props

At least a week before strike, call the people from whom you rented any props and make appointments for the props' return. The golden rule of renting props is: Return the props in the same condition as when you first rented/borrowed them. Restore these items to their original condition and return them with the same (or better) care you demonstrated when first taking them into your temporary possession. Be thorough, return the correct props to the right person, and make each return happen in one trip. Constantly calling someone to tell them you've "found yet another one" of their things is not acceptable.

Before you put props back into your department's prop storage make sure they are clean and in good shape. Wash dishes and soft goods and wipe off paint or dirt used for distressing props. Return props to storage in a timely manner, making sure each prop is placed back in its correct section.

Props that are show specific and could not be used for another production, such as specialized paper props and food goods, can be thrown away. Any props that are damaged beyond repair can also be pitched.

Closing Budgets

Once a show has been closed and struck, the budgets for those shows can also be retired. Record outstanding receipts, fill out your reimbursement and purchase order forms, and turn all of it into the finance department. Your supervisor may ask you to provide other information as well.

Chapter 10
Safety

"These fumes make me nauseous!" Protect yourself when you work! Be safe. Handle chemicals and tools carefully. Know what is toxic. Be prepared with first aid supplies should accidents happen. A prop master needs to be knowledgeable about handling weapons and special effects and all union, state, and federal laws that affect props. Everything matters in the world of theater.

Proactive Protection

Take Care of Yourself

The prop master hats you don are physically demanding and mentally draining. Take care of yourself. Eat properly and often. Sleep properly and often. Don't burn the working candle at both ends (except on rare occasions). Listen to your body — it will tell when you've pushed yourself too hard. When you are tired, rest.

Theater is a creative art, but most professional and serious artists don't have time for using substances that can alter their judgment. You can't afford the risk of not being in control of all of your faculties while at work. Refrain from alcohol and drugs while propping.

First Aid

First Aid Kits

Every prop shop should have a fully stocked first aid kit that is readily accessible. The kit should hang on a wall, close to a

bathroom, where nothing will cover it up or be stacked against it. No matter how messy the shop may become, there should always be a clear path leading to the kit.

Keep the first aid kit stocked. There are companies who will stop by every month or so to check on the stock and replenish supplies. If you decide to stock the kit yourself, be diligent about it.

First aid kits are stocked with many things beyond gauze pads and finger bandages. Use this list as a guide to help you get your kit up and running.

First aid kit supplies:

Ace bandages	Adhesive tape
Antibiotic ointment	Anti-diarrhea medication
Antiseptic wipes	Aspirin
Bandage strips	Calamine lotion
Cold packs	Cotton balls
Finger splints	Gauze pads
Hand sanitizer	Hydrocortisone cream
Hydrogen peroxide	Ibuprofen
Isopropyl rubbing alcohol	Needle
Oral antihistamine	Saline solution
Scissors	Thermometer
Triangular bandage	Tweezers
Vinyl disposable gloves	

First Aid and CPR

Every prop master should be trained in CPR and first aid. All theater technicians should be trained in these procedures. In the United States, the Red Cross and YMCA have training sessions every week. The cost of training should be covered by the theater; if not, the personal expense is worth it. First aid includes many different skills for temporarily treating someone who is injured. Burns, wounds, and broken limbs do happen in the prop shop and need immediate care while waiting for professional medical care. CPR, or cardiopulmonary resuscitation, is administered to someone whose heart has stopped and/or is no longer breathing. Chest compressions and mouth-to-mouth ventilation will keep the blood flowing through the body, but most likely will not restart the heart. CPR should be performed until professional help arrives or the victim begins to breathe on his own.

MSDS

There are over three million Material Safety Data Sheets (MSDS) designed to provide the correct procedures for working with potentially hazardous products and substances. Your MSDS collection can be kept in a binder but must be accessible in the shop to all employees. These sheets provide information on what the substance or chemical is and data about the substance, including what the dangers are, first aid administration, how to store the substance, and what protective equipment to wear. What I've mentioned here is not a complete list of all the information an MSDS contains; it is only an overview. The length of a typical MSDS is at least four pages per chemical.

Anyone who works with certain chemicals on a regular basis or who may come in contact with the hazardous substances at work should read the MSDS. The sheets can be ordered from many sources online. Only the sheets that pertain to the chemicals found within the prop shop need to be ordered; otherwise you would have six million sheets cluttering your shop, creating more confusion than necessary.

Warning Labels

Common household products do not need a MSDS. However, every cleaning supply, adhesive, paint, stain, and stripper has hazard and health warnings on the container. Follow these warnings and the directions for use. It is worth the time. When you are working with many products, ventilate your work space and try to use only one product at a time. If you must use multiple products, make sure the chemicals aren't mixed. Clear the room of the previous vapor before using another product. Vapors, alone or mixed, can have serious effects on your health — either immediately or over time.

Use your MSDS to learn how to work properly with various products. For example, a popular carving medium in theater is Polystyrene. This simple looking material can produce toxins that seriously affect the human nervous system.

Polystyrene Warning

When working with Polystyrene (more commonly known as Styrofoam), it is worthwhile to take health precautions.

Polystyrene emits the vapor Styrene, which irritates the eyes, nose, and throat and has adverse affects on the human nervous system. If you use heat to carve or cut this foam, it will release the vapor. If you simply carve the foam, you will create polystyrene dust. Use steps to protect yourself and others. Work in a well-ventilated workshop. Wear a respirator and safety goggles.

Physical Safety

Accidents

Accidents are bound to happen. It doesn't matter how many preventive measures you take or how careful you are; you will get a splinter, smash your finger, get sawdust in your eye, and need a finger bandage from time to time. For more serious accidents, call the emergency number for an ambulance and remain calm, especially if you are only the witness to the accident. Have you ever noticed how calm the victim in an accident usually is compared to how his injuries suggest he should be acting? It is usually the onlookers who are freaking out. Don't lose your cool if someone is injured. You have first aid training, so you know how to minister to the injury. The same pertains to a circumstance when you are the injured person. Keep your wits about you and you will be able to handle any situation.

When someone at work has been seriously injured, medical aid should be sought and the production manager or supervisor should be alerted. Businesses need to have a record of the accident for insurance purposes. Normally, Workman's Compensation will supply insurance coverage and monetary compensation for work that may have been missed as a result of the injury. An accident report form should be filled out no matter how serious the injury. An innocent slip one day could result in serious back pain a week later. If the accident is not reported, Workman's Compensation will not be granted. Your theater should have an accident report form similar to the one in figure 10.1.

ACCIDENT REPORT FORM

REPORT ALL CLAIMS TO INSURANCE COMPANY WITHIN 24 HOURS!

PLEASE PROVIDE COPY OF REPORT TO BUSINESS OFFICE IMMEDIATELY

NAME OF INJURED: _____

HOME ADDRESS: _____

_____

_____

HOME PHONE #: _____

CELL PHONE #: _____

DATE OF BIRTH: _____

SOCIAL SECURITY #: _____

JOB TITLE: _____

PART TIME: _____ FULL TIME:_____

DATE OF ACCIDENT:_____

ACTIVITY AT TIME OF INJURY: _____

_____

DESCRIPTION OF INJURY: _____

_____

MEDICAL ATTENTION SOUGHT? YES _____ NO _____

AMBULANCE RIDE REQUIRED? YES _____ NO _____

WITNESS AT TIME OF ACCIDENT: _____

FOR BUSINESS USE ONLY:

DATE RECEIVED:_____ POLICY #: _____

Figure 10.1

Tool Safety

When you are working with power tools, simple precautions will keep you safe. No matter how comfortable you are with tools, they can still be harmful. If you are afraid to use a power tool, ask someone to assist you. While fear will keep you aware of your surroundings, it can also be paralyzing.

Here are standard safety reminders for working with power tools:

- Do not wear loose-fitting clothing; remove all jewelry.
- Keep long hair tied back and all hair out of face and eyes.
- Keep your shoes tied.
- Check that the power cord is in good condition; have it fixed if it is not.
- Wear eye protection, ear protection, and respirators or dust masks.
- Keep the shop floor free of dust and debris.
- Draw knives away from your body; the same rule applies when using chisels.
- Before using a saw, check your surroundings to ensure your workspace is clean and clutter free.
- While using a saw, be conscious of where fingers and body parts are in relation to the blade.
- Use the tool for the purpose for which it was designed, and know how the tool will operate before using it.
- Do not use power tools near liquids or flammables.

Ladders should only be used in the manner for which they were designed. Balancing an extension ladder on top of an A-frame ladder is incredibly dangerous, but I have seen it done. Make sure all latches on the ladder are secure before climbing. Wear shoes and use your hands to help you climb. Know your own strength when lifting and setting a ladder in place. If you need help, ask for it. These tips may seem obvious, but they are reiterated for a reason: not enough people follow them.

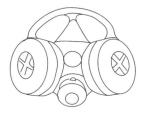

Shop Protective Gear

You can't have a workshop without tools, and you shouldn't work in your shop without having the proper stock of protective gear. Every professional prop and/or scene shop should have the following protection items on hand:

Chemical suits	Disposable vinyl gloves
Dust masks	Ear protection
Eye wash/eye wash station	Fire extinguishers

Goggles
Leather or cotton gloves
Respirators
Steel-toed shoes
Welding apron
Welding screen

Hard hats
Metal cabinets
Rubber gloves
Welding mask
Welding gloves

Dust Collection System and Spray Booth

Most scene shops and large prop shops are starting to install dust collection systems and spray booths. Dust collection systems pull airborne dust particles created from working with wood and other materials into filters so that employees don't have to breathe in the particles all day long. The systems also cut down on the amount of sawdust that accumulates on the shop floor.

Spray booths can range from a hood ventilation system to specially designed spaces as large as rooms. These booths remove the toxins from the air created by chemicals like spray paint, stain, strippers, and most cleaners.

Weapons and Special Effects

Firearms

If it is absolutely necessary to use and fire a real gun on-stage, then *only* blank ammunition should be purchased and used. Never aim a gun at anyone, including the audience, regardless of whether it is loaded, not loaded, a starter pistol, or able to fire real bullets. If the weapon is not being fired, the firing pin should be removed as a precaution. One crew member should be responsible for cleaning and loading the gun, distributing the weapon to the actor, retrieving the weapon as soon as it is through being used, and locking it up again. Guns should be cleaned before each use, and each chamber should be filled with blanks in case the gun misfires the first time.

Starter pistols are used frequently in theater, especially when a gun is discharged offstage. These pistols have a distinct look and only use blank ammunition because the end of the barrel is purposely blocked. Starter pistols do not have a completely realistic sound, but using them is better than accidentally harming someone.

No matter what kind of gun is used on-stage, it should be treated like a weapon, and all precautions should be adhered to.

To reiterate, here are common-sense gun safety rules:
- Do not load the gun until right before it is to be used, and unload it immediately after use.
- Use the appropriate sized blanks for the gun, otherwise it will malfunction.
- If you are unsure if the guns in your stock actually fire, take them to the experts — the people who legally sell guns — and have each gun inspected.
- Learn how to operate the gun. The experts will be willing to teach you.
- Clean the gun before use. Make sure it is unloaded first.
- Fill all chambers of the gun with blanks before firing.
- Never point a gun at someone. If firing a gun for sound effect purposes, aim the gun towards the ceiling as you extend your arm up past your head.
- Wear ear protection and safety goggles. Do not discharge the gun near your body — the paper wadding from blank ammunition could still penetrate your flesh.
- Do not hold the gun with your finger on the trigger.
- Lock the gun up when not in use.
- Never use a prop gun to pull a prank on someone.

Other Sharp or Dangerous Props

All prop weapons should be treated with care. If the prop is a real-life weapon or could be used as a weapon despite its role as a stage prop, it should be given special treatment. Pocket knives, kitchen knives, swords, axes, maces, nightsticks — the list of weapons is endless. All prop knives, or anything with sharp, knife-like edges, brought on-stage and used by actors and crew should have dull blades. You can dull a knife blade by giving it a few passes on the bench grinder. If you do not have one of these, a sharpening stone and sandpaper designed for metal sanding are acceptable substitutes.

Locking Up Weapons

It is good practice to lock up all weapons regardless of whether they really shoot, crush, or slice. If weapons are locked up and out of sight, people with curious hands won't be tempted to touch them.

Locking up weapons takes the guesswork out of your job. You will always know where the props are; their safety and yours will never be in jeopardy.

State Regulations, AEA Rules, and Common Sense

Before you hunt down a gun, start planning for special explosive effects, or even just think about running a fog machine, you will need to do some research. Your supervisor may already know what AEA, or the Actors Equity Association — the labor union for professional actors and stage managers — has to say about what kind of effects you can produce on-stage. State laws may prohibit certain effects at certain venues, and common sense will help you pick out the best effect from what remains on the list.

Pyrotechnics and People

Don't make an actor perform a dangerous or even somewhat harmful trick or effect if you are not willing to try it yourself. If you don't try the trick beforehand, how can you know if it works correctly and safely? How will you show the actor how to use the effect in performance if you don't know yourself? Safety first. The companies that supply special effects to theaters always promote safety. The people who work at these companies want you to put together effects with their products in the safest way possible while creating the most appropriate effect. These experts will also suggest products that will protect the operator from injury. Before you assume that you can handle effects on your own, think again, and seek out expert experience and advice.

Smoking and Fire Safety

Smoking

Noel Coward's plays will have to start being performed outside without an audience once every state adopts no-smoking laws. It used to be that herbal cigarettes could replace tobacco cigarettes on-stage after states banned smoking from indoor public places, including theaters. But herbal cigarettes produce the same toxins in the air as tobacco, so these herbals are being banned too. What's a prop master to do? If your theater is producing a play in which smoking on-stage is necessary, the first thing you should do is check with your state to see if this is legal. If it is not, tell your supervisor and artistic director and let them decide if they want to risk paying a fine and/or being shut down — at least they will know where the law stands.

If smoking is allowed on-stage, (cigarettes, cigars, pipe, and "other,") provide the actors with the mildest kind of herb or tobacco available. Ashtrays should be heavy in weight so as not to be tipped over easily. They can be secured with Mortite or rolled up gaff tape. You will want them to be removable so you can empty and wash them. Fill a small portion of the bottom of the ashtray with clear dish or hand soap. Soap will help extinguish the cigarette or cigar and won't evaporate under the heat of stage lights. Place a convenient can of sand on each side of backstage for when an actor comes offstage with a still-lit cigarette. A fairly deep amount of sand will snuff out the cigarette.

Warning the Audience

The audience should be aware that actors will be smoking before they enter the house. The house manager is responsible for creating and displaying warning signs, and the stage manager usually informs the house manager of who will smoke and when. Audience members should be allowed a ticket refund if they have to forego seeing the show because of smoke allergies — but that is for the box office and theater organization to determine, not the prop master.

Fire

Before you even consider having live flame on-stage — even it if it is just to light a match or candle — equip your stage with up-to-date and working fire extinguishers. Better yet, before any performance or stage rehearsal, have the theater check the maintenance and location of the fire extinguishers.

Using actual flame on-stage is a dangerous hassle. You'd think it would be easier to light a candle than to spend hours making a battery-operated candle that will never look completely real no matter how talented the artisan. But live flame poses so many dangers that it is not even worth considering.

However, there will be plays that cannot use battery-powered substitutes. If candles must be used, they must either be pillars wide enough to stand by themselves or be properly secured in a candle holder. Torches can be made using Sterno fuel carefully disguised and lit right before it comes on-stage and extinguished the second it leaves the stage.

Most theater curtains are flame proof. Fabrics and paints should be treated with flame proofing, and every precaution should be taken to prevent the slightest mishap. Lighting one candle on-stage takes weeks of planning, preparation, materials, and labor, whereas a battery-operated candle takes only a few dollars and a few hours to construct.

Chapter 11
Timeless Tips and Techniques

"I made this!" The "basics" of prop creation may seem obvious and simple to some, but these prop techniques are timeless. Industry and technology will continue to change and offer new materials and tools to work with, but certain ways of woodworking, sewing, and distressing materials have stayed with us through the ages. They will always remain the same, and they will always be needed.

This chapter is not intended to solve all your prop-building concerns. Quick tips are just a tantalizing taste of how endless the crafting possibilities are in the propping world. If you need more guidance with crafting props, check out the resource section at the back of this book. There are many good books listed that focus solely on crafting special props. How-to books that tell you how to do specific things are some of the best resources.

Building Simply

Flats/Platforms

Flats are the walls of a set. Their size varies in width and height. There are two types of flats used in theater: soft flats and hard flats. **Platforms** are walked on and act as the floor of the set. They can also be used to visually enhance the design of the set and break up the picture by adding different levels of acting space. Rarely will the prop master build flats or platforms, but the basic building techniques for these elements can be applied to many prop projects. And it never hurts to be a well-rounded member of the production team.

Soft Flats

The least expensive way to build the walls of the set, soft flats are comprised of a wooden frame with fabric (typically muslin) stretched and secured over the frame. Soft flats are lightweight and travel well when handled carefully. The fabric should be primed or starched before being painted; this gives it a stiffer surface and keeps the paint from soaking in and seeping through the fabric. A water-based paint can be used as a primer, or flats can be primed with starch. If your soft flat is to be translucent, starch is the recommended primer.

Hard, or "Hollywood" Flats

Hard flats are built similar to the framing of soft flats, but the wood is set on edge rather than flat. The difference is that the frame is not covered with fabric; a sheet of material like luan is used instead, which makes the hard flat more sturdy. When these flats are upright and the edges are seen, the thickness of the stile can give the illusion of the depth of a constructed wall. Although these are a tad more expensive to build and heavier to maneuver, they are the preferred method for flat construction and set construction. Hard flats closely resemble the surface of walls in a building; they are easier to paint and texture, and set dressing can be attached with screws or nails.

Assembling the Frames

Putting the frames together is fairly simple construction. Pine boards measuring 1 x 4" are cut to the required measurements and assembled "laying down" on the flat face of the boards. As demonstrated in Figure 11.1, the top and bottom rails sandwich the side stiles into a frame. A toggle is added in the middle to provide extra support. The cut edges of the stiles are glued before being sandwiched, and the corner blocks and keystones are attached with screws to keep the pieces together and to keep the corners square.

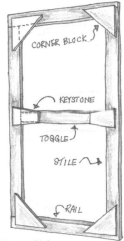

Figure 11.1

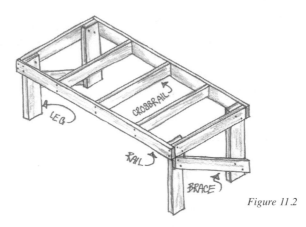

Figure 11.2

Platforms

Platforms are normally built using 2 x 4" pine boards cut to design specifications and assembled as in figure 11.2. Platforms usually have legs to give them height and help distribute weight. Crossrails act as supports for the plywood board that is attached horizontally to the top of the framing. Braces are added to keep the legs straight; they are usually attached at an angle for extra support. The pieces are glued together using wood glue and then screws or pneumatic staples or nails are used to permanently attach the pieces together.

Tables

Tables are a regularly-used stock piece of the prop department. The construction can be simple, faked to look more complex, or tables may be properly constructed. When you take the time to properly construct a table, it will be sturdier and last longer.

> **Work Tables**
> Platform construction can be adapted into the perfect 8' x 4' x 40" work tables.

Basic Styles

There are two very basic styles of table that are easy to construct and can work for a variety of period and size needs. The construction is the same for end tables, coffee tables, dining tables, and sofa tables; it is only the size that varies.

Any of the styles shown in figures 11.3, 11.4, and 11.5 can be used in rehearsal, but it is the mortise and tenoned construction, seen in figures 11.4 and 11.5, that usually makes it to the stage.

154

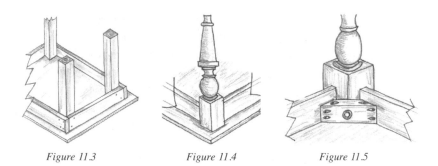

Figure 11.3   *Figure 11.4*   *Figure 11.5*

Figure 11.3 is an upside down view of quick table construction. 1/2" to 3/4" plywood works best as the table top. Posts measuring 4 x 4" or laminated 2 x 4" pine boards create sturdy legs, and the apron (the rails that connect the legs and provide support) can be 1 x 4" pine boards or something similar. Glue and then screw the pieces together, then sand and paint, and it is ready for rehearsal.

A mortise and tenon-style table construction can be faked. In the proper construction, the tenon is like a tongue crafted into the cut edges of each apron piece and glued into the hole, or mortise, cut in the top of the leg in the same size as the tenon. To make it simpler, the aprons can butt up against the top of the legs and be held in place using corner irons attached to the apron and the underside of the table. Corner blocks or corner leg braces can create the hypotenuse by connecting the aprons together. A bolt through the middle of the corner block will hold the leg in place until the table top can be glued and screwed permanently in place from the top. This construction works best if the table will be painted rather than stained because the screw holes can be filled and then sanded.

Benches

Benches are a standard prop. It seems like you can never have enough of them in enough different styles. Figure 11.6 provides an example of a quick way to build a sturdy little rehearsal bench. Half-inch plywood can be used as the seat and 1 x 3" pine boards do well for the legs and stretchers.

Figure 11.6

Figure 11.7

A slightly more complex bench that could be destined to adorn a rustic setting can be seen in figure 11.7. The wide legs and top of this bench can be pine board or plywood. The middle stretcher is a 2 x 4" pine board.

Once sanded and screwed together, these benches will last for much too long, and you will beg your prop master friends to take them off your hands so you can begin a new bench collection.

Quick Crafting Tips: Beverages and Food

Liquids

Liquids are a favorite prop because the action of drinking gives an actor something to do and a chance to quench his thirst while performing. Really — why else are drinks requested?

Champagne Glasses

When actors have to drink champagne, a great substitute is ginger ale. It bubbles nearly the same, the cork will pop off the champagne bottle when shaken, and the coloring is perfect.

Musicals like to torture waiter characters/ dancers/actors by having them dance while carrying full champagne glasses on a tray. To avoid spillage, a light amber-colored gel from the electrics department, set inside the glass, will trick the audience into thinking the glass is full of champagne. See Figure 11.8. This trick also works for glasses "filled" with red or white wine.

Figure 11.8

Liquor

Dark-colored liquors can be made by brewing tea bags into a dark tea potion, then diluting the tea until you see your desired color of prop liquor. As you dilute, have a clear glass of the real liquor handy so you can compare the two drink colors. Water, obviously, works for clear liquors; juices or food dye can stand in as wines.

Beer

The easiest way to make prop beer is to use recycled beer bottles, stripped of their old labels and adorned with newly crafted replicas of vintage beverages. Fill the bottles with warm ginger ale or lemon-lime soda and recap them with a bottle capper (available at kitchen stores).

Beer cans are trickier, especially if the cans need to be opened on-stage, and *especially* if the pop tops aren't pop tops, but the old fashioned peel backs. But making beer labels to cover soda cans is fairly simple — just a little computer crafting and researching pictures and the job is done.

Foods

Prop food can be crafted out of just about anything, as long as it is not to be eaten. These props are also fun to create. Lots of materials craft fake food quite nicely, especially if you don't have a budget to buy pre-made artificial foods. Clay, polystyrene, spray foam, casting resin, sponges, upholstery foam, shammies, and Model Magic® are great materials to start with. Spray insulating foam makes nice cream puffs, muffins in a tin, or bread in a bread pan. Be careful — this kind of foam expands to almost triple its size.

Real food dries out too quickly for theater use and reuse. Obviously a real fruit salad won't even last one performance because it will turn completely brown. Pasta will dry up within a day, and breads and cookies will dry out and become too brittle for stage use.

Steer clear of putting a clear coating of shellac over things that rot in an effort to preserve them for the run of a show. It may be urban legend by now, but a long while ago, a friend of mine told me that he worked on a production in need of a Cornish hen or two as a hand prop that was never consumed. Instead of crafting one, the prop master coated a real roasted chicken with shellac and, once performances started, forgot all about the prop. After many nights of sitting under the heat of the stage lights and days upon days of sitting in the open air, the roasted hen exploded during the middle of the dinner scene. Apparently there was no carcass in the carcass — only the skin had been preserved, and it was so beyond rotten that they had to stop the show until the smell cleared the auditorium.

I love that story — true or not.

Specific Techniques

Aging and Distressing

Both aging and distressing are staple techniques for the prop department. You can use modern means to craft almost all things antique.

Aging

Paper props are very prevalent in shows, and they are especially fun to make when you can play around with aging techniques. To make parchment, all sorts of paper will work: craft or butcher paper, thin typing paper, or even copy paper will suffice. Crinkle the paper, then moisten and gently tear the edges a little. Un-crinkle the paper and flatten it out a bit, then dunk it in a pot of hot tea bags. The more tea bags you use, the darker the outcome. After the paper has soaked for a while, pull it out and let it dry completely. Once it is dry, take a warm iron to it and smooth out the wrinkles. Now it should be ready for whatever other application you need to add to it.

Design Master® Glossy Wood Tone, a floral spray paint found at craft stores in the floral crafting sections, is a quicker way to turn paper old. The spray does exactly what the name says — it give items a nice wood tone. On paper, the "gloss" does not show up as much because you are just "spritzing" your paper.

Reflections/De-shining

Prop tech notes are sometimes full of "please dull that down," or, "the mirror was moved offstage until you can make it less reflective." So what are good prop techniques for making something dull and less shiny? There is a product called Dulling Spray which puts a permanent coat of a slightly frosty matte finish on your projects. If you are able to permanently dull something down, a frost spray or even quick and light spritzes of gray, black, or brown spray paint will do the trick. Vaseline smeared in even coats will keep an object from reflecting a lot of light, but will also make it look blurry.

Tools for the Techniques

Very few props escape the torture of being distressed once they are marked that way in the design. Other ways in which prop masters can age and distress:

- Watery washes of brown/gray/black paint will tone windows and create a unified look of places that are worn out, old, dusty, and slightly mildewy.
- Sandpaper in the grit appropriate for the task can wear down paint or stain on corners of furniture or chair seats.
- Chains, when whipped onto wood, make realistic indentations that represent years of use and abuse. This is especially nice for distressing farming implements and old wagons and crates.
- By sawing off bits of your props here and there, the jigsaw can add years to the age of your items. Just be careful not to take too much off the top
- Rasps/files work very well on fabrics to give them a nice worn or pilled look.

More Stuff

Color On-Stage

Color is not just an element of design to make a production visually stimulating and bring the concept to life. Color is tricky because it can change right before your eyes when it goes on-stage. The way color affects props sometimes puts limits on what props you acquire for the show. White will look almost as bright as a fluorescent color under stage lights because it bounces the light right back. Even lighter creams will look like bright white on-stage. Black can look like burgundy or dark blue depending on of the type of black dye mixed with the color choices of the lighting crew. When you are propping and concerned about color choices, perform color tests under stage lighting to see what the final look has the potential to be.

Stage Directions

Understanding stage directions and how the stage space is divided will help you excel in your job and be able to effectively communicate with other theater artists and technicians.

Typical Prop Sizes

- Seat height for most chairs is 18" from the floor.
- A prop's "footprint" is the outside measurement of the area of space the item takes up on the floor.

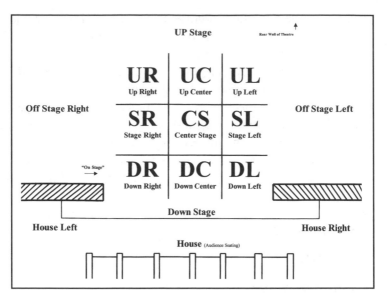

• The average dining room table measures 30" high; end tables are anywhere from 20" to 24" tall; coffee tables are 18" tall.
• Shelves are spaced anywhere from 10" to 12" apart within a unit and are no deeper than 12".

Basic Sewing Stitches

Hand sewing is another trade of the prop shop. There are four very common stitch patterns that are easy to do and can serve different purposes.

Running Stitch

The running stitch is the most basic and can be used as a seam or a gathering stitch. After threading your needle, hold your fabric together with one hand, push your needle through the side of the fabric facing

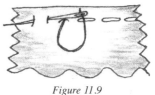

Figure 11.9

you, through the opposite side, and repeat from the opposite side back to your side. Or you can hold the needle relatively in the same spot and fold the fabric back and forth like an accordion over the end of the needle, then pull the needle through the fabric. Try to keep the stitches fairly even. Stitches that are smaller and closer together will create small gathers when the thread is gently pulled taut. Longer stitches spaced farther apart will create large gathers.

Back Stitch

The back stitch is the strongest hand stitch, which a sewing machine replicates. This would be used if you didn't have access to a sewing machine and needed to

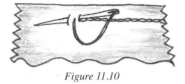

Figure 11.10

repair soft goods with a strong bond. Start out creating a running stitch and, after two stitches, make a stitch backwards that fills in the space between the two initial stitches. After that, for every running stitch forward, take one stitch back.

Whip Stitch

The whip stitch is a quick and dirty way of attaching two edges while also helping to keep the materials from unraveling. This can produce a rather unsightly seam if the stitches are not kept even. See figure 11.11.

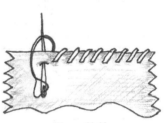

Figure 11.11

Hidden Stitch

The hidden stitch will make lighter-duty seams look like they were machine sewn. The needle starts this stitch from inside the crease of one piece of material. It is pulled through the fabric, crosses

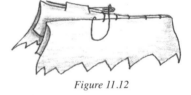

Figure 11.12

over to the other fold of the fabric, and disappears into a hole exactly opposite of the one it just came out of. The needle then travels along the inside of the fabric crease, perpendicular to the actual stitch it just made, and reemerges an eighth of an inch down the cross, only to cross back over to the original side and disappear again. When perfected, this stitching method pulls two fabrics together and the thread completely disappears from view.

Drafting Lines and Symbols

These are the most important drafting lines to a prop master. There are many more lines and standard ways in which to draw and communicate how props and set pieces should be built. The ten most basic drafting lines appear in figure 11.13.

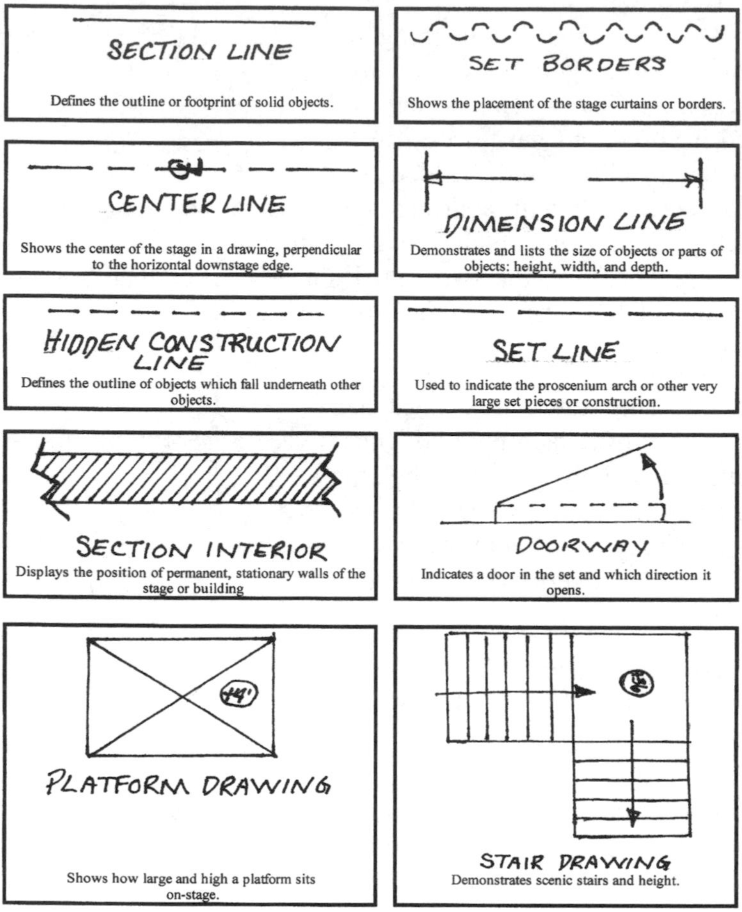

SECTION LINE

Defines the outline or footprint of solid objects.

SET BORDERS

Shows the placement of the stage curtains or borders.

CENTER LINE

Shows the center of the stage in a drawing, perpendicular to the horizontal downstage edge.

DIMENSION LINE

Demonstrates and lists the size of objects or parts of objects: height, width, and depth.

HIDDEN CONSTRUCTION LINE

Defines the outline of objects which fall underneath other objects.

SET LINE

Used to indicate the proscenium arch or other very large set pieces or construction.

SECTION INTERIOR

Displays the position of permanent, stationary walls of the stage or building

DOORWAY

Indicates a door in the set and which direction it opens.

PLATFORM DRAWING

Shows how large and high a platform sits on-stage.

STAIR DRAWING

Demonstrates scenic stairs and height.

Figure 11.13

Basic Theater Terminology
A Glossary of Sorts

Theater "speak" or terminology is usually standard with every theater or venue. Being a knowledgeable, well-rounded theater member will not only make you look good while you're doing your job, but will also keep you aware of your surroundings and safe while maneuvering on-stage. When a co-worker yells "Heads!" you'll know to seek cover. The more you know, the better off you'll be.

A

Action: The term for movement on-stage.

Acting Areas: The various areas on the stage or set in which actors may move and be seen by the audience.

Aircraft Cable: Thin, strong, steel cable frequently used in theater for flying heavy scenery.

Apron: Part of the stage projecting into the auditorium in front of the house curtains.

Antique: A generalization that an object or thing is old-fashioned or related to the "days of yore."

Armature: A skeletal form that is the framework for materials which flesh out the desired shape.

Aside: Lines spoken by an actor to the audience, not to other actors and not noticed by other actors/characters on-stage.

Auditorium: The area of the theater building where the audience sits to watch the show.

B

Backdrop: See Drop.

Backstage: Areas of the stage behind and to the sides of the set which are not seen by the audience.

Bar/Batten: Horizontally flown pipe from which scenery, lighting, and other equipment are hung.

Base Coat: The first of several coats of paint or layers of texture for a drop, scenic piece, or prop.

Barn Door: Lighting term for a piece of equipment with adjustable shutters which can be attached to lighting instruments to help shape the beam of light in an acting area.

Black Box: A small, single-level, intimate theater space with flexible stage or audience seating spaces.

Blacks: A group of leg and border curtains used to define space on-stage and conceal the wings and backstage areas.

Blackout: The period of darkness during a show used to define the end of one scene and the beginning of another.

Bleed Through: When an image or light can be seen through what is otherwise supposed to be opaque.

Blocking: Instructions given to actors to stand or move about the stage at specific times.

Boom or Light Tree: A vertical lighting pipe with small pipe arms clamped to it. Supports several light instruments.

Border: A horizontal curtain or piece of hard scenery trimmed to hide lights and flown scenery from the audience.

Bounce: Stage light that hits an object and bounces or is reflected back; light-colored objects will make light bounce and look brighter than they actually are.

Box Set: A stationary set depicting a room minus the fourth wall.

Braces: Wooden supports fixed to flats and screwed or weighted to stage floor.

Budget: The amount of money available to use in procuring items for a production.

Build: To construct or make something as in costumes, props, scenery, and light and sound cues; the process of creating.

C

Cable: Long wires encased in rubber with connectors at each end. Specially designed for providing power to lighting instruments or transferring power or signals to sound equipment.

Call: A notice of the time at which actors or technicians will be required to report for work; instructions given by the stage manager to the crew during a performance.

Callboard: A cork board located backstage on which daily calls, schedules, and all other information relevant to the production is posted.

Call the Show: The duty of the stage manager during the performance to call out the light, sound, and scenic cues over the headset.

Canvas: A strong piece of cloth prepared as a surface for painting.

Carriage: The part of a stair unit that supports the tread and risers.

Cartooning: The process of transferring outlines from painter's elevations to scenery or a drop.

Catwalk: A narrow walkway or bridge suspended above the house and used for lighting positions.

Center Line: An imaginary line running along the stage, upstage to downstage, equal to the midpoint of the proscenium arch.

Chalk Line: String wound in metal case, saturated with colored chalk. When stretched tight and snapped onto a surface, it will produce straight lines. Also called a Snap Line.

Closing Night: The last performance during the run of the show.

Commando Cloth: A lightweight cotton fabric suitable for stage drapery, similar to felt on one side; also known as duvetyn.

Come Down: Instruction to move an object or an actor downstage towards the audience.

Concept: The overall creative idea or theme for a production.

Contact Sheet: List of all people working on a production, their titles, and how best to stay in touch with them during the rehearsal and performance periods.

Costume: Clothing an actor wears during a performance to help portray a character.

Cornerblock: A triangular-shaped piece of thin, sturdy wood used to reinforce the joint between a stile and a rail of a flat.

Corner brace: A length of wood placed at a diagonal inside the frame of a flat to help keep it square.

Counterweights: A permanent system of ropes, wire lines, weights, and pulleys used for raising and lowering flown scenery.

Crash Box: A hand-held solid wooden box filled with metal and plastic objects that when shaken or thrown produce a crashing sound effect.

Crew: Group of theater technicians who work together on a specific aspect of theater production.

Cross-Fade: To "seamlessly" fade or change light intensity from one acting area to another.

Crossover: The space actors and technicians use to get from one side of the stage to the other without being seen by the audience; usually located upstage and behind the set or backdrop.

Cue: Signal for an actor to enter or speak a line; point at which a lighting, sound, or other effect takes place during the show.

Cue Light: Small box with lights hidden from audience that turn on or off to warn actors or technicians of impending business.

Cue to Cue: Rehearsal of technical effects in a production with actors, one cue at a time.

Cure: Time required for adhesives to harden and reach full strength.

Curtain: End of show.

Curtain Call: Actors reappearing at the end of the play to bow, give thanks, and receive audience applause.

Curtain Speech: Pre-show address to audience by a cast member or theater staff.

Curtain Time: The proposed start time of the performance, as advertised.

Cut: To remove something permanently from the show, such as a scene or technical element.

Cut In: To paint or cut material close to a line.

Cutter: A person who cuts the material for costumes based on specific patterns.

Cyc: A large, usually white backdrop, hung at the rear of the stage and lit as needed.

D

Dark: A theater that is temporarily closed between production periods.

Dart: A short seam used to make material look tailored and fit more snuggly against an object.

Deck: Floor area of the entire stage.

Decking: A walkable covering or surface of a platform or floor.

Distress: To change new fabric, wood, or metal to look old, worn, or aged.

Dolly: A small, wheeled platform used to move or load-in heavy scenery.

Downstage: The area of the stage closest to the audience.

Draping: The process of creating a pattern for a specific costume.

Dresser: A stagehand who assists actors with their costumes throughout the run of the show.

Dress Rehearsal: The rehearsal period usually after technical rehearsals and before opening night designed to use all technical elements of the performance and run the entire show without needing to stop.

Drop: A rather large painted piece of canvas (usually a landscape) hung vertically to the stage and considered a scenic element.

Dry Run: A rehearsal without actors to test and improve tech elements.

Dutchman: A thin piece of material glued over the seam between two flats in an attempt to make the flats look like a large solid wall.

Duvetyn/Duve: See Commando Cloth.

E

Elevation: A picture drawn accurately and to scale, showing the side view of scenery pieces or light systems.

Escape Stairs: Stair units connected to an upstage portion of a set that allows actors to exit second-story scenery without being seen by the audience.

Extra: An actor with no lines who serves as a member of the crowd.

F

False Proscenium: Hard flats or curtains placed right behind the real proscenium arch for decoration or to help minimize the visual size of the arch and stage space.

Feedback: An annoying sound coming from speakers and sound system; also, thought or input in response to an activity or project.

Find the Light: To place oneself within the hot spot of a lighting instrument or area of lights.

Fire Proofing: To treat fabric, wood, or other highly porous and flammable materials with a chemical flame retardant.

Fire Curtain: A specially made (and installed) fire-resistant curtain that will seal off the stage from the house in case of fire. Also known as a Safety Curtain.

Fiscal Year: A period of twelve months used with businesses for reviewing and computing annual financial statements.

Fitting: A meeting of costume staff, designer, and actor for trying on costumes and taking notes on necessary changes.

Fixture: Another term for a lighting instrument.

Flat: Standard unit of scenery made of a wooden frame (stiles, rails, and toggles), covered with stretched fabric or hard wood and vertically supported with jacks or braces.

Flies/Fly Space: The area above the stage to which scenery and lighting battens are flown.

Flown: Scenery or lighting equipment either suspended or "hidden" in the flies; can appear on-stage and is controlled by a counterweight or pulley system.

Fly: The process of bringing scenery in and out of the stage area vertically using a counterweight or pulley system.

Fly In: A command for bringing battens or scenery out of the flies and to the stage area.

Fly Out: A command for pulling battens into the flies.

Focus: The process of adjusting each stage lighting instrument's beam to shine in the exact area to be lit on-stage.

Fog: "Cloud-like" substance heavy enough to hug the ground. The effect is usually created by vaporizing dry ice in hot water in a specially designed machine.

Follow Spot: Light directed at and intended to follow an actor across the stage.

Foot: Placing one's foot at the bottom edge of a flat or something that needs to be raised vertically; holding a ladder steady and in place with your feet and body weight.

Footlights: Lights placed along the downstage edge of the stage to up-light the set and actors.

Footprint: The surface area an item covers.

Fourth Wall: Imaginary wall between audience and actors which would complete or close off a room if it were a realistic space.

Front of House (FOH): The lobby, box office, and concession areas of a theater.

G

Gaff Tape: A strong, cotton cloth, adhesive tape used as a multi-purpose tool or material; also called Gaffer's Tape.

Gel: Specially developed colored film that can be placed within a lighting instrument to project different colors onto the stage.

Ghost Light: A standing lamp set at center stage and turned on when the stage and auditorium will be empty of people and dark for any length of time.

Glow Tape: A self-adhesive tape that glows in the dark and is used to mark platform or furniture edges so they can be found in blackouts.

Go: Spoken only by the stage manager during a performance to give stage hands the cue of action.

Gobo: Thin metal plate with a cutout shape that slides into a special slot of a lighting instrument to create interesting shapes and designs on the stage or set.

Going to Black: A warning from electrics or stage management to actors and other technicians that the stage will be thrust into pitch blackness.

Grand Rag: Slang for the large, usually ornate curtain that closes off the opening of the proscenium arch.

Greenroom: Common area with certain amenities where actors and technicians hang out during performances.

Grid: Metal pipe hung in a grid pattern above the apron area on which lighting instruments, speaker clusters, and occasional scenic pieces are hung.

Grommet: A strong metal ring punched through fabric in order to reinforce the holes for hanging.

Ground Plan: A detailed scale drawing of the set and prop placement given from a bird's-eye view; also known as Floor Plan.

Ground Row: Long sections of short standing scenery usually placed upstage; intended to hide floor-mounted lighting instruments or other equipment.

H

Half Hour: A warning call from stage management given to the actors and technicians half an hour before they will be called to the stage for the beginning of a performance.

Hang: The process of hanging lighting instruments and cable to battens, booms, catwalks, and grids.

Hazer: A machine that can fill the entire stage with a mist or fog.

Hanging: Attaching set pieces, instruments, or equipment to battens.

Header: A small flat that is placed between two flats to create a doorway or window.

Heads: A warning called out by those who have just dropped something or witnessed something dropping from a height that could endanger those below.

Heads Up: A notification; a warning of an impending activity.

Head Set: Term referring to individual components of a communication system allowing the appropriate production staff to communicate with one another during the show.

Heard/Thank You: A response in reply to an instruction, time, or danger warning.

Hold: A call, usually given by the stage manager or director, to stop or pause the action of play without the actors and technicians straying too far from position.

House: Everything beyond the stage; usually the areas where the audience is allowed within the theater building.

House Curtain: The main curtain in a proscenium theater. See also Grand Rag.

House Left: All areas of the house that are positioned to the audience's left.

House Right: All areas of the house that are positioned to the audience's right.

Hue: The qualities that differentiate various levels of what is categorized as the same color.

I

IATSE/I.A.T.S.E.: International Alliance of Theatrical Stage Employees; a union for theater stage hands and technicians.

In Place: An actor who is in position for an entrance or the beginning of a scene.

Intermission: The ten- to fifteen-minute breaks between acts of a play.

J

Jack: A triangular support that holds a flat in a vertical position. See Braces.

Jog: A flat less than two feet wide.

K

Keystone: A rectangular piece of wood used to strengthen and cover the joint between the stile and toggle bar of a flat.

Kill: To shut down a light, lighting system, or other equipment.

L

Lamps: Specially designed bulbs used in theatrical lighting equipment.

Legs: Black, narrow curtains hung vertically to mask the wings and backstage areas.

Levels: Ramps, steps, and platforms which create various acting areas at heights above the main stage.

Light: A source that makes vision possible in a dark area.

Light Plot: A computerized or hand-made scale drawing detailing the location of every lighting instrument used in the production.

Lines/Line Sets: Ropes and systems for raising and lowering scenery and lighting battens in and out of the flies.

Load-In/Load-Out: The moving of scenery and equipment into or out of the theater and stage.

LORT: League Of Resident Theaters; promotes the welfare of and provides support for resident theaters regarding union and government relations.

Luan: Thin, strong, and rather flexible sheet of wood commonly used for covering flats or other surfaces.

M

Masking: To hide the backstage area from audience view with curtains or other scenery.

Material: Supplies used in crafting or building.

Model (Set): A small-scale, 3-D representation of what the set and its components will look like when finished and installed on-stage.

Model Box: A small-scale, wooden box designed to mimic the theater space, stage, walls, etc., in which a set model will be placed.

Mood: A distinctive atmosphere provoking certain emotions or feelings.

Monitors: Speakers placed around the stage in order for singers or actors to hear themselves. Monitors are used in dressing or greenrooms for actors and technicians to listen to the performance on-stage.

Muslin: A flat-surfaced, woven cotton fabric that comes in varying weights and can serve different purposes.

N

Notes: Remarks and requests for improving and altering specific technical or acting elements of the production as deemed necessary by the director, designers, and stage management. A notes session usually follows a rehearsal or preview performance.

O

Off Book: Referring to an actor who no longer needs to rely on his script during rehearsals.

Offstage: A reference to nearby backstage areas when on-stage.

On Book: Referring to an actor who still needs to reference his script for lines during rehearsal.

On-stage: Any area of the stage that is visible to the audience.

Open Up: To turn something so that it mostly faces the audience.

Opening Night: Traditionally known as the first night of a performance in front of an audience; usually highly celebrated.

Orchestra Pit: A recessed area located at the front of the stage, in between the house and the stage, usually lower than the stage, where the orchestra performs.

OSHA: Occupational Safety and Health Administration; an American federal agency which issues and enforces health and safety standards in the workplace for the prevention of illness and injury.

P

Pack the House: An effort to fill the auditorium with as many paying audience members as it will hold.

Paper the House: An effort to give away tickets in order to make a performance appear to be selling better that it is.

Painter's Elevations: Renderings of the set painted to show colors and painting styles to be used on the actual set.

Performance: A formal presentation of a play, story, or other exhibition.

Personal Props: Small hand props that are specific to one character and carried throughout the show.

Pilot Hole: A tiny hole drilled into a piece of wood to hold the tip of a screw or drill bit.

Places Please: The verbal phrase from stage management signaling the cast and crew to report to their positions for the start of the performance.

Platform: A horizontal playing space of any size, elevated to a specifically designed height by strong legs.

Plot: A description of the action of the play.

Plywood: Laminated layers of wood to create strong, heavy-weight sheet material used in building construction.

Practical: An electrical or mechanical prop that appears to perform the same job on-stage as it would in real life.

Preset: The predetermined placement of scenery, props, and costumes before the start of every show; a lighting cue designed to illuminate the set as the audience takes their seats.

Preview: A rehearsal performance for paying audience members before Opening Night.

Production: The process of giving life to the words of the script via rehearsals and the realization of design elements.

Production Meeting: A weekly gathering of appropriate theater department managers, designers, and director used to discuss and plan for the needs of the show and pass along information.

Production Team: Technical theater professionals who work together to make important decisions regarding the show.

Professional Theater: Any theater that pays its staff, actors, and guest artists to design, build, and perform a show.

Program: The booklet or brochure handed to audience members before each performance containing information pertaining to the show and those involved.

Prompt Book: The stage manager's copy of the script with detailed blocking records as well as call placements for light, sound, and scenic cues.

Proscenium Arch: The structural stage opening which separates the actors from the audience.

Properties (Props): Any item provided for a performance that does not fall under scenery or costumes.

Props Table: A table placed offstage with designated sections to set and replace props during a performance.

Pull: To find and take an item from a certain stock or storage area for use in a production.

Pyrotechnics: Special effects that involve electrical charges, fire effects, smoke, flashes, etc.

Q

Quick Change: A very quick costume change that takes place close to the side of the stage.

R

Rail: A top or bottom piece of wood that helps frame out a flat.

Rake: A stage or set of platforms with an incline where the higher end is upstage and lower end is downstage.

Read-Through: A rehearsal in which the play is read without action or blocking.

Rendering: A drawing portraying what the set, props, and costumes are supposed to look like when completed.

Rigging System: A network of lines, pulleys, and battens used for hanging scenery, much like a counterweight system.

Riser: Another term for platform; the vertical portion of a stair unit.

Run: Entire length of calendar time the play or show will be performing or available for viewing,

Run Lines: A method of memorization while practicing a character's scripted words with another person.

Run-Through: A rehearsal of the play from beginning to end.

S

Safety Chain: Chain or thin cable used to clip around a batten and yoke of a lighting instrument to provide backup safety support.

Safety Curtain: See Fire Curtain.

Sand Bag: A canvas bag filled with sand and used to add weight to fly systems or anything else that needs counterweight.

Scenery: Specially designed and built scenic pieces which create the environment that supports the play and action.

Scrim: A drop made with large-weave material that can be opaque or transparent depending on the lighting design.

Sectional: A scale drawing of a scenic piece or prop as if cut in half and looked into from the side.

Set: The scenery and props assembled on-stage exhibiting a dimensional environment for the characters and the story of the play.

Set Dressing: Props used to decorate a setting.

Sheet Goods: Building materials such as wood, foam, or plastic that are made into flat panels several feet wide and long; can be up to an inch in thickness.

Sheer: A thin, translucent curtain to hang in front of a window to filter light.

Shift Rehearsal: A rehearsal for stage management and stage crew, without actors, to learn and practice the cues and choreography of scene shifts.

Sightlines: Imaginary lines that test the audience's view of visible areas on-stage.

Slipstage: A platform big enough to hold the entire set.

Smoke Machine: A machine which uses a special fluid that, when heated, can produce smoke that fills the air or area but dissipates quickly.

Snap Line: See Chalk Line.

Soft Goods: A term used in theater to describe stage curtains, drops, materials, and props such as textiles, bed linens, towels, curtains, etc., that are made from fabrics with no rigid structure.

Spattering: A process that adds dimension to painted surfaces by controlling the splatter of tiny paint droplets either with a sprayer or by slapping a paintbrush against one's hand.

Speaker: Piece of sound equipment placed about the house which allows the audience to hear the sound from the stage.

Specials: A light used for isolating an area or highlighting a moment in the performance.

Spike: A mark made to indicate the position of a set or furniture piece on-stage.

Spike Tape: Thin gaff tape in different colors, used in small pieces to make a spike.

Spill: Used mostly to describe stage light that is unintentionally falling or bleeding into an area in which it was not designed or focused.

Stage: A specific area designated as the playing space for performances.

Staging: The movements of an actor during the action of the play.

Stage Business: Things actors do or movements they make on-stage to have their character come across as more realistic.

Stage Crew/Stage Hands: Name for theater technicians who work with specific technical aspects either backstage or unseen by the audience during the run of the show.

Stage Directions: Instructions found within the script to describe the movements of the characters and action within the story.

Stage Door: The backstage or rear theater entrance usually used by production personnel and guest artists.

Stage Floor: The deck of the actual stage, minus any set.

Stage Screw: A large hand screw used to tie a moveable scenery piece to the stage floor temporarily.

Staged Reading: A performance of a play on a bare stage in which the actors use minimal movement while still holding the script to deliver lines.

Stage Weight: Cast-iron weight intended to work in a counterweight system; doubles as weights for many theater purposes.

Stage Whisper: A spoken line loud enough for the audience to hear, but giving the illusion of a purposeful whisper.

Standby: A warning given by stage management to stage crew over headset that a cue is imminent.

Steal the Scene: To shift the focus of the audience when it is supposed to concentrate on something else in the scene.

Stile: The long, wooden, vertical side framing of a flat.

Stitcher: A person who sews and puts together all the fabric pieces of a costume.

Stock: Materials, clothing, furniture, or items kept by a theater in storage for future use or rental.

Stock Set: Scenery kept in stock for reuse which usually depicts a general location.

Strike: Instruction to remove an unwanted item from stage; the event for dismantling and removing all of the technical elements of the production after the run is over.

Swag: Fabric gathered together and hung so that it drapes differently than normal curtains.

Swatch: A rectangular fabric sample to show what material to use for a prop or costume.

T

Tech (Technical Rehearsal): A time in which all technical aspects of the production are introduced, rehearsed, and refined.

Techie: Nickname for a stage technician.

Technical Production: The organizing, maintaining, designing, crafting, and building of all technical aspects of the production departments for theater performances.

Texture: The type of surface composition that affects smoothness or coarseness.

Theater: Building where shows are performed; also a term to reference this particular performance art.

Theater in the Round: An auditorium and stage in which the audience sits on all sides of the playing area.

Thespian: A follower of the Greek actor Thespis; an actor.

Thunder Sheet: A large sheet of steel that, when suspended and shaken rapidly, will produce a thunder-like sound effect.

Thrust Stage: Stage in which the audience sits around three sides of the playing space, with the fourth side serving as backstage.

Tie Line: Black, covered, thin cotton rope used to tie curtains or cable to battens; has proven to have multiple uses.

Toggle/Toggle Bar: A horizontal piece of lumber centered in a flat to connect the stiles and offer additional support.

Tone Down: To soften the shade or quality of a color or object; to reduce its brilliance.

Trap: A hole cut in the stage floor, concealed by a door, and used for special effects or entrances and exits.

Trim: Scenery or masking hanging parallel to the stage at a specific height as needed by the design of the sets and lights.

Truck (Wagon): A platform on casters; used for creating movable scenery pieces.

Turnbuckle: A metal rod with threads and links at both ends; used for tightening lines used in hanging scenery.

Turn In/Turn Out: To turn one's body toward or away from others.

U

Upstage: The area of the stage that is toward the back wall and farthest from the audience.

Upstaging: A prop placed upstage that brings attention to itself and causes the props further downstage to "look bad." Or, an actor standing upstage of the other cast members causing the entire cast to look upstage and therefore turn their backs to the audience.

Unit Set/Fixed Set: A set in which little to none of the scenic elements move or change position during the show.

Uplight: Light placed below or beneath actors to provide extra illumination.

USITT: United States Institute of Theater Technology.

V

Value: Lightness or darkness of a particular object.

Velour: A thick, heavy material with a deep pile; used for upholstery and drapes.

Vintage: Something of certain interest or quality which is recognized as being from a particular period of origin.

W

Wagon: See Truck.

Walk-On: A small acting role with no lines.

Walk-Through: Time taken from the beginning of tech rehearsals for actors to walk around and test newly added scenic elements.

Walk Up: A careful way of transferring a horizontal flat or piece of furniture to a more vertical or upright position.

Wardrobe: An offshoot of the costume department that maintains the cleanliness, inventory, and integrity of the costumes used in performances.

Warn: Based on the preference of the stage manager, using the word "Warn" is similar to saying "Standby."

Wash: The covering of an area with a thin coat of translucent paint in order to tone down or soften an image or color or to make transparent material more opaque.

Wash-Out: When the color and definition of an object disappears because of the brightness of the stage lights.

West Coast: The process of bundling up a suspended backdrop and tying its entirety to the batten at one foot intervals so it can be flown out of sight.

Wings: The areas adjacent to either side of the stage right and stage left acting areas, hidden from the audience's view.

Work-Through: A rehearsal process in which specific technical and acting elements are rehearsed repeatedly until perfected.

Bibliography and Resources

Here is an abridged listing (just a sampling, really) of books to assist Prop Masters with hunting, gathering, communicating, building, and creating theatrical props. The more you know, the better off you are.

Bibliography

Dover Publications, Inc. New York. http://www.doverpublications.com.

The Merriam-Webster Dictionary. Springfield, MA: Merriam-Webster, Incorporated, 2004.

Campbell, Drew. *Technical Theater for Nontechnical People*. New York: Allworth Press, 2004.

Carter, Paul. *The Backstage Handbook*. Shelter Island, NY: Broadway Press, 1994.

Crabtree, Susan and Peter Beudert. *Scenic Art for the Theater*. Burlington, MA: Focal Press, 2005.

Davies, Gill. *Create Your Own Stage Effects*. New York: Backstage Books, 1999.

Gillette, Michael. *Theatrical Design and Production: An Introduction to Scenic Design and Construction, Lighting, Sound, Costumes and Makeup*. New York: McGraw-Hill, 2007.

Holt, Michael. *Stage Design and Properties*. London: Phaidon Press Limited, 1994.

Ionazzi, Daniel. *The Stagecraft Handbook*. Cincinnati, OH: Betterway Books, 1996.

Kaluta, John. *The Perfect Stage Crew*. New York: Allworth Press, 2003.

James, Thurston. *The Theater Props Handbook*. Studio City, CA: Players Press, 1990.

Sweet, Harvey. *Handbook of Scenery, Properties, and Lighting, Vol. 1*. Needham Heights, MA: Allyn and Bacon, Inc., 1994.

Segaloff, Nat. *The Everything Etiquette Book*. Avon, MA: Adams Media Corporation, 1998.

Wilson, Andy. *Making Stage Props: A Practical Guide*. Wiltonshire: The Crowood Press Limited, 2003.

Resources

Aronson, Joseph. *The Encyclopedia of Furniture*. New York: Crown Publishers, Inc., 1961.

Heimann, Jim, ed. *All American Ads* (Series). Spain: Taschan, 2003.

Isreal, Fred, ed. *1897 Sears, Roebuck Catalogue*. Philadelphia: Chelsea House Publishers, 1968.

James, Thurston. *The Prop Builder's Molding and Casting Handbook*. Cincinnati, OH: Betterway Books, 1990.

Lord, William H. *Stagecraft 1*. Colorado Springs: Meriwether Publishing Ltd., 2000.

Marx, Ina Brosseau, Allen Marx, and Robert Marx. *Professional Painted Finishes*. New York: Watson-Guptill Publications, 1991.

Miller, Judith. *The Style Sourcebook*. New York: Stewart, Tabori, and Chang, 1998.

About the Author

Growing up in Prairie Village, Kansas, Amy Mussman fell in love with theater performance at the age of six when she participated in her first acting class at Theater for Young America in Kansas City. As time went on and her family moved to Frederick, Maryland, her passion for theater only grew stronger. An active thespian, Amy spent much of her high school years examining both the backstage and acting arenas while participating with school, church, and community theater groups and a local children's theater touring company.

Amy received a Bachelor of Arts degree in Theater from Kansas State University and spent her college years studying light, costume, and set design. After graduation, she began her first professional theater season at Delaware Theater Company as production assistant and worked as prop master for nine seasons. She has enjoyed a decade of summers as either the costume designer for Allenberry Playhouse and Forestburgh Playhouse, the prop master for Maine State Music Theater, or working as an instructor and director for Delaware Theater Company's summer youth theater camp.

Working on freelance projects fills many of Amy's extracurricular passions for writing and crafting. She has also spent her free time designing costumes and sets for high schools in the Delaware and New Jersey area. "Focusing on being a well-rounded, knowledgeable theater artist or technician," Amy says, "will not only make you a confident team member, but will keep the art of theater forever interesting and challenging — opening all doors to creativity and imagination."

About the Illustrator

Photo by: Phyllis Mussman,
Mussman Group Creative Services

James Mussman is a freelance computer graphics artist, 3D modeler, and web designer currently residing in Frederick, Maryland.

James recently obtained his degree in Computer Graphics and Interactive Media at the University of Dubuque, Dubuque, IA. While at Dubuque, James received multiple Student Ad awards from the Ad Club of Dubuque, which is part of the American Advertising Federation. He also won awards for artwork in the University of Dubuque Art Show.

As a freelance artist, James has designed projects for the Delaware Theatre Company and the Grand Opera House of Dubuque, published an image in the *Articulate*, the University of Dubuque art and literary magazine, and has created several professional websites.

Order Form

Meriwether Publishing Ltd.
PO Box 7710
Colorado Springs, CO 80933-7710
Phone: 800-937-5297 Fax: 719-594-9916
Website: www.meriwether.com

Please send me the following books:

_____ **The Prop Master #BK-B301** $19.95
by Amy Mussman
A guidebook for sucessful theatrical prop management

_____ **Introduction to Stage Lighting #BK-B270** $19.95
by Charles I. Swift
The fundamentals of the theatre lighting design

_____ **Stagecraft I #BK-B116** $19.95
by William H. Lord
A complete guide to backstage work

_____ **Self-Supporting Scenery #BK-B105** $17.95
by James Hull Miller
A scenic workbook for the open stage

_____ **Instant Period Costumes #BK-B244** $19.95
by Barb Rogers
How to make classic costumes from cast-off clothing

_____ **Costuming Made Easy #BK-B229** $19.95
by Barb Rogers
How to make theatrical costumes from cast-off clothing

_____ **Costumes, Accessories, Props and** $19.95
Stage Illusions Made Easy #BK-B279
by Barb Rogers
How to make costumes, accessories, props and stage illusions

**These and other fine Meriwether Publishing books are available at
your local bookstore or direct from the publisher. Prices subject to
change without notice. Check our website or call for current prices.**

Name: _____ e-mail: _____

Organization name: _____

Address: _____

City: _____ State: _____

Zip: _____ Phone: _____
  ❑ **Check enclosed**
  ❑ **Visa / MasterCard / Discover / Am. Express #** _____

Signature: _____   Expiration
                                       date: _____ / _____
        (required for credit card orders)

Colorado residents: Please add 3% sales tax.
Shipping: Include $3.95 for the first book and 75¢ for each additional book ordered.

  ❑ *Please send me a copy of your complete catalog of books and plays.*